Construction is a Team Sport

Errol Lawson

EWL Consultants

"The strength of the team is each individual member. The strength of each member is the team."

— Phil Jackson, former NBA coach

Contents

Praise for Construction is a Team Sport

As academics, we often remind our students that education is not only about acquiring knowledge but also about developing the character and skills that allow that knowledge to be put to good use.

Nowhere is this clearer than in the construction industry. Technical competence will always be necessary, but it is the human dimensions of communication, collaboration, and resilience that transform competence into excellence.

Construction is a Team Sport speaks directly to the realities of professional practice within the construction industry. Errol Lawson has produced a timely and significant text that not only prepares students, apprentices, and graduates for the transition into the workplace but also empowers them to succeed and flourish once there. The book engages openly with the challenges often faced by newcomers—uncertainty, lack of confidence and the sense of being different from peers—and reframes these experiences as opportunities for personal and professional growth. In so doing, Lawson provides readers with strategies to communicate effectively, collaborate productively, and exercise leadership with integrity.

A key strength of this book is its openness. It directly addresses long-standing cultural barriers in the construction sector, such as rigid hierarchies and the underrepresentation of women and minority groups. At the same time, it offers practical and inclusive ways to overcome these challenges,

emphasising that the future of construction will depend on the meaningful contributions of diverse

voices.

For educators and trainers, this book addresses a long-standing gap. While our curricula have traditionally emphasised technical ability, they have often overlooked the interpersonal, behavioural, and leadership capabilities that employers consistently identify as critical. Construction is a Team Sport bridges this gap, proving how communication, teamwork, and emotional intelligence elevate technical competence into professional excellence.

I recommend this book to all who are entering or advancing within construction. It is both a guide to practice and an invitation to help build an industry that is more collaborative, equitable, and resilient.

— Professor Mujib Rahman PhD CEng PGCHE FICE FCIHT FIAT SFHEA Head, Department of Civil Engineering Aston University Birmingham, United Kingdom

I really enjoyed this book. It's not the usual dry career guide — it feels more like someone cheering you on and giving you real, practical advice you can actually use. Errol Lawson talks openly about the challenges of working in construction, especially if you're new or feel like you don't quite fit in, but he does it in a way that's encouraging and down-to-earth. The mix of stories, tips, and straight talking makes it easy to read and easy to apply. I came away feeling more confident about how to handle myself on site and in teams. Definitely a book I'd recommend to anyone starting out in construction.

— Randeep Sami Vice Principal James Watt College

Construction is a team sport' is a well-researched and written book that provides valuable advice across a broad range of relevant topics. It is recommended to anyone considering a career in the built environment – no matter what age.

— Mark Harrison Head of Equality, Diversity and Inclusion Transformation - CIOB

Construction is a Team Sport is an inspirational guide to the human side of construction. Errol Lawson shows how confidence, communication, teamwork, initiative and emotional intelligence can help young professionals grow and succeed. A must-read for building careers and teams, this book is practical, motivating and full of genuine insight. I highly recommend it to those at the start of their careers and employers who want to build stronger and more effective teams.

— Siu Mun Li Most influential woman in construction 2024

I highly recommend Construction is a Team Sport for anyone entering the industry, especially those who feel like they don't quite fit the traditional mould.

It goes beyond technical skills to highlight what truly drives success in construction: communication, emotional intelligence, and the courage to lead authentically.

Welldone you for producing another masterpiece!

— Charlene Wall CEO Wood Manor Properties

In a time where this sector is not just on the rise but also crying out for new and diverse talent, Errol tackles perfectly the barriers that often hold people back from entering and achieving their true potential.

Through the book you will feel yourself submerged in first day nerves and revisiting times of self-doubt. Using his skill and inside knowledge and reflecting on personal experiences, Errol offers an impeccable vision to guide you through these emotions and provides a unique toolkit to navigate success. Although written to boost confidence in relation to entering the construction industry, this book is so much more. This is a life manual that will serve you in so many situations, this will become your "go-to" in the times you question yourself and need to up the volume of your positive inner voice."

— Jayne Hanson Solihull Council

Construction is a Team Sport by Errol Lawson is a powerful and inspiring read that highlights the importance of collaboration in the construction industry. Lawson, a trailblazer in creating opportunities for young people, shares practical insights and real-world examples that emphasise teamwork, leadership, and accountability. This book is a must-read for anyone passionate about building not just structures, but also futures.

It's both a guide and a call to action for inclusive, purpose-driven change in construction."

**— Lee Davies Head of Operations
United Infrastructure**

Construction is a Team Sport is a thoughtful and accessible book that addresses the people side of the construction industry with clarity and passion. Errol Lawson has perfectly captured the essence of the essential soft skills needed to thrive in the construction industry, or indeed many other professional environments.

His insights are practical, inspiring, and grounded in real-world experience. This book is not just about building careers; it's about building a stronger, healthier, and more inclusive industry. I would particularly recommend it to young people embarking on a career in construction, as well as educators and employers.

— Eddie Hughes BEng MCIOB Hughes Housing Consultants (Former Housing Minister)

Errol Lawson has identified something the construction industry desperately needs to hear collaboration isn't just a nice-to-have—it's the foundation of success. In Construction is a Team Sport, he makes a compelling case that technical brilliance means little without the human skills to coordinate, communicate, and build trust across diverse teams. What impressed me most was Errol's practical honesty about the real barriers young professionals face, which he then follows up with actionable strategies for developing the confidence, emotional intelligence, and initiative that will help them become indispensable team members. It's well known that poor communication undermines project delivery, so the emphasis in the book on collaboration as a core professional competency is critical. This book is a blueprint for building not just structures, but the high-performing, collaborative teams that are the future of construction.

— Andrew Geldard Chief Communications Officer Willmott Dixon

Construction is a Team Sport is a practical guide for the next generation entering our industry. Errol's focus on teamwork, communication, and confidence equips young people with the skills they need not only to succeed but to thrive. At a time when improving diversity and inclusion is vital, this book provides both encouragement and practical tools to help every individual – regardless of background – find their place and make an impact.

— Professor Rosa Wells

Construction is a Team Sport is a powerful guide to the people side of construction. Errol Lawson highlights five essential skills—confidence, communication, teamwork, initiative, and emotional intelligence—offering practical insights for young professionals. A must-read for employers, educators, and anyone entering the industry.

— **Claire Kershaw** CEO Social Infrastructure, United Infrastructure

Construction is a Team Sport" is a refreshing and much-needed perspective for the construction industry. Errol Lawson masterfully uses the metaphor of sport to create a compelling narrative that truly resonates with young professionals, inspiring them to take ownership of their growth and careers. This book is more than a guide; it's a practical toolkit filled with principles that help bridge the gap between technical ability and the soft skills that underpin real success. Errol's work reminds us that competence isn't just about what we know, but how we lead, communicate, and collaborate. A must-read for both early-career and seasoned professionals who want to build meaningful, sustainable careers in construction to help our communities thrive!

— **Raynee De Zoysa** Senior PM at CAA ICON

Foreword

When people think about construction, they may picture cranes on a skyline, hard hats and boots on muddy, cold sites, or the blueprint of a building that will one day become a school, a bridge, or a home. What fewer people see—at least at first—is that behind every project, behind every structure that shapes the world around us, there is something far more powerful than concrete and steel: people.

Construction is, at its core, a team sport. It is thousands of interactions, conversations, and decisions—big and small—made by people who must find ways to collaborate, respect each other, and bring out the best in one another. And yet, for too long, we've treated "soft skills" as optional, as though technical knowledge alone is enough to succeed in this industry. It isn't. Buildings may be made of bricks, but careers are built on relationships, trust, communication, and courage.

This book, Construction is a Team Sport, is a particularly important contribution to help young people step into this industry not just with competence, but with confidence. It's written for those entering construction professions—apprentices, graduates, trainees—and especially for those who may feel the industry wasn't built for them. If you are a woman, a person of colour, or someone from a background that looks different from the majority you meet on site, then this book speaks directly to you. But it also speaks to every one of us who wants to make construction a more inclusive, respectful, and forward-thinking industry.

The author brings a unique voice to this subject. Errol is a true leader, and a trailblazer by instinct, he hasn't had an easy path. His own background is marked by challenge and resilience. He understands, in his bones, what it takes to walk into a new place for the first time feeling like an outsider—and what it takes to stay, thrive, and lead. That authenticity makes this book far more than a manual; it is a mentor between covers.

What sets this book apart is its honesty about the realities of construction. Yes, the work is rewarding, creative, and vital. But the industry also carries pitfalls —cultures that can slip into negativity, hierarchies that can silence good ideas, and banter that sometimes crosses the line into bullying. Too often, people new to the sector are told to "toughen up" or "fit in," instead of being encouraged to bring their full selves to the table. This book tackles that old thinking head-on. It shows you how to find your voice, draw your boundaries, and call out behaviour that diminishes others—without losing your place on the team.

You will find here practical lessons in professional communication: the art of active listening, clarifying before assuming, interpreting what's really being said. These are not abstract theories. They are the daily habits that will make you a trusted colleague, the kind of person people want to work with again and again.

You will also discover insights into mindset—the quiet but powerful force that shapes how we approach challenges. Construction will test you. There will be long days, pressure, and setbacks. But there will also be breakthroughs, camaraderie, and pride. Developing resilience without becoming hard, ambition without arrogance, humility without self-doubt—these are the balances that matter. And this book equips you to find them.

One of its strongest themes is courage. Courage to speak up. Courage to take chances. Courage to back yourself when you doubt you belong. For women and minorities in a white male-dominated sector, this is especially crucial. Representation in construction is improving, but progress is slow, and the weight of being "the only one" in a room or on a site can be heavy. This book gives you permission not only to take your place but to take it proudly.

And courage, of course, must be matched with emotional intelligence. The ability to read the room, to sense when a colleague needs support, to know when to push and when to pause—these are the marks of true professionals. They create the psychological safety where teams flourish, where mistakes are admitted early rather than hidden, and where innovation can thrive.

Equally important are gratitude and positivity. The author reminds us that while the industry is changing, every one of us plays a role in shaping its culture. By avoiding negativity, recognising others' contributions, and lifting those around us, we all become custodians of a better construction industry. Culture is not abstract—it is what we do every day.

Throughout the book, real examples bring these ideas to life. You will read about team who stumbled and recovered, teams that pulled together under pressure, and individuals who made choices—sometimes small, sometimes brave—that changed the outcome for everyone. These stories will remind you that construction is never a solo pursuit. We succeed, or we fail, together.

For anyone starting out, one of the most valuable chapters will be on taking initiative and understanding boundaries. Knowing when to step up and take responsibility—and when to respect the limits of your role—is a fine line. Get it wrong, and you risk either being invisible or overstepping. Get it right, and you build credibility that will carry you forward. This book shows you how.

I am especially struck by how this work bridges the gap between technical training and behavioural development. Our apprenticeship programmes, university courses, and professional qualifications are strong on the technical —how to calculate, design, or deliver—but they rarely teach the interpersonal. Yet ask any seasoned leader in construction what makes the biggest difference on site, and they'll tell you it's not the blueprint. It's the people. The greatest projects are built by teams that communicate, trust, and support one another. That is why this book is such an important addition to our learning landscape.

For educators, trainers, and employers, Construction is a Team Sport deserves a place alongside the textbooks and the technical manuals. For students, apprentices, and graduates, it should be a companion you carry from your first day on site to your first day as a leader. It provides what so many curricula miss: the behavioural elements that transform competent individuals into exceptional professionals.

But above all, this is a hopeful book. It recognises that while construction has a long way to go in becoming more inclusive and collaborative, the future belongs to those willing to shape it. Every young person who reads this has the chance to be part of that shift—to be not just a participant in construction, but a pioneer of its culture.

So as you open these pages, know this: you are not just entering an industry. You are joining a team. And that team needs your voice, your presence, your courage, and your kindness. The buildings we create will stand for generations.

The culture we build together will determine what kind of industry, and what kind of world, those generations inherit.

This book will help you play your part.

— Deborah Madden, Executive Director – CITB

About the Author

Professor Errol Lawson is the founder of the *Building the Future Awards* – a pioneering programme celebrating and developing the next generation of construction professionals. The awards recognise young talent across the UK construction sector, highlight innovation, and create opportunities for training, mentoring, and leadership development. For more information, visit www.buildingthefutureawards.co.uk.

An award-winning entrepreneur, leadership coach, and author, Professor Lawson holds an honorary Professorship and Fellowship at **University College Birmingham**, recognising his outstanding contribution to leadership, education, and industry development. With over a decade of experience across construction, education, and business leadership, he has trained and inspired professionals at every level – from apprentices to senior executives.

Known for his dynamic teaching style and practical insights, Professor Lawson combines academic expertise with real-world experience, holding a Level 7 qualification in Strategic Leadership and a Master's degree in Enterprise Management.

Through his books, workshops, keynote talks, and industry initiatives, his mission is simple: to help the next generation of construction professionals build not only remarkable projects but also resilient, collaborative, and future-ready careers.

Introduction

Walking onto a construction site for the first time as a young professional can be both exciting and over-whelming. You might be eager to apply your technical skills, yet also keenly aware of the unfamiliar environ-ment around you. Perhaps you notice you're one of the youngest people on the team – or one of the few women or people of colour in sight. That feeling of standing out is real: women make up roughly 11–14% of construction workers, with some sources citing around 11–12% [1][2][3]. Representation in construction management is even lower, with women accounting for approximately 8.79% of the workforce in 2023 [4][5]. Similar underrepresentation exists for many minority groups; for instance, Non-Hispanic Blacks held only 5.1% of construction jobs in 2020, despite making up 12.6% of the overall U.S. workforce [6][7]. In the UK, the representation is equally low: only 5.4% of construction workers come from Black, Asian, or other minority ethnic backgrounds—notably less than the 13.8% they comprise within the broader UK population [8].

In such a traditionally male-dominated, hierarchical arena, it's natural to wonder, "Do I belong here?" or "How can I earn respect and prove myself?" Take heart: you are not alone in these thoughts, and yes, you do belong. This book, *Construction is a Team Sport*, was written for you – the aspiring or rising construction professional who's ready to meet these challenges head-on. We understand the very real hurdles you face. It's not just the steep learning curve of technical know-how; it's the subtle people dynamics of the construction site. It's walking into a meeting where everyone else is older – or walking onto a site where someone like you is a rare sight – and still finding your confidence and voice. It's encountering attitudes that might underestimate you and deciding to turn that around through your performance and character. These are real challenges, and this introduction wants to acknowledge them upfront. But more importantly, we're here to tell you that these challenges can become opportunities once you harness the right skills and mindset.

Here's a well-kept secret: long-term success in construction isn't determined solely by how much technical knowledge you have or how well you can calculate load-bearing capacities. In fact, research shows that only about 15% of job success in the long run comes down to technical competence, whereas a whopping 85% of success depends on "soft" skills [9] [10]. Surprised? Think about it – a project may be built with steel and concrete, but it's held together by people. As is often said in the industry, the construction industry relies on the strength of its workers "not the physical strength – but strength of character." Your work ethic, integrity, communication, and ability to connect with others are the true backbone of sustained achievement on site. Mastering those people-centric skills is like discovering a superpower in a field that has historically put technical ability on a pedestal. It gives you a competitive edge to excel in an industry where many of your peers might still assume that technical know-how is all that matters.

Fortunately, the industry is waking up to the importance of these skills. A recent large-scale survey of construction professionals found that 87% believe soft skills play an important role in effective construction practices – with 68% saying they have a very important role. In the same study, about 69% of respondents admitted there's a noticeable shortage of these soft skills in our sector [11]. In other words, there is a growing recognition that communication, teamwork, adaptability, and emotional intelligence aren't just "nice-to-have" extras – they are critical competencies that many in the workforce are missing. Employers are increasingly seeking well-rounded people who can collaborate, lead, and problem-solve, not just operate machinery or crunch numbers. As new technologies, client expectations, and project complexities reshape construction, the ability to work well with others and navigate human dynamics is more vital than ever.

One early-career recruitment manager put it bluntly:

"We can easily teach you technical skills. It is harder to teach you the interpersonal skills you need to succeed – and we can't teach you the work ethic that gets you out of bed in the morning."

In a hiring process, you may find that your attitude and people skills are what set you apart from other candidates with similar technical qualifications. The message is clear: technical skills may get your foot in the door, but people skills are what will carry you upward.

That's where *Construction is a Team Sport* comes in. The purpose of this book is to serve as your practical guide to mastering the "soft" side of construction – the people and communication skills that will amplify everything you do. Within these pages, we'll walk through core skills and habits that will help you build credibility from day one and become a highly valued team member on any site. You'll learn how to project confidence (even when you're the least experienced person in the room), how to communicate like a professional with colleagues, clients, and crews, and how to collaborate in a team so that others genuinely enjoy working with you. We'll discuss taking initiative in a smart way – showing leadership potential and resourcefulness without overstepping – and we'll delve into developing emotional intelligence, so you can stay cool under stress, navigate conflicts, and read the room effectively.

In short, *Construction is a Team Sport* will help you become more confident, a strong communicator, a team player, proactively resourceful, and emotionally intelligent in the workplace. These are learnable skills, and each chapter will break down concrete techniques and real-world examples to help you practice and grow.

Above all, this book is about empowering you. It's about helping you realise that by honing these people skills, you're not changing who you are – you're becoming more of who you were meant to be as a professional. The construction industry is competitive and can be tough, yes, but that means there's huge opportunity for those who rise to the occasion. By developing your soft skills, you'll quickly set yourself apart. You'll find that co-workers start coming to you for advice on coordinating with others, or that your manager trusts you to handle a delicate client interaction. That's credibility. That's influence. Over time, those are the qualities that get you promoted and open doors to leadership.

There's an often-cited adage in career development: "Hard skills get you hired; soft skills get you promoted." Studies even suggest that employees with stronger soft skills tend to earn higher wages and advance further in their careers – because they excel at the human side of getting results [12][13][14]. The ability to communicate, lead, and empathise gives you a reputation as someone who can not only do the job, but help improve how the whole team does the job. In an industry that's striving to improve safety, efficiency, and innovation, such a reputation will make you indispensable. Simply put, becoming "site smart" about people is one of the smartest investments you can make in yourself.

Let's also address a myth head-on: the idea that great people skills are innate – that some folks "just have it" and others don't. This is false. The truth is every expert was once a beginner, every confident leader you see was once a nervous newcomer. Skills like communication, leadership, and emotional intelligence can be learned, practiced, and improved by anyone with the willingness to try. As author Brian Tracy wisely said: "Communication is a skill that you can learn. It's like riding a bicycle or typing. If you're willing to work at it, you can rapidly improve the quality of every part of your life" [15].

Want to Go Further?

This book is just the beginning. If you'd like to take your development to the next level, we run a range of **workshops, training courses, and leadership programmes** designed specifically for people working in the construction industry. These sessions are practical, interactive, and focused on the very skills that will help you thrive in your career – from communication and teamwork to leadership and resilience.

You can also discover more about the **Building the Future Awards**, which celebrate and showcase the rising talent shaping the future of the built environment.

To find out more about our **construction training courses, workshops, and awards**, visit:

www.buildingthefutureawards.co.uk

References

National Association of Home Builders (NAHB) (2024) *About NAHB*. Available at: https://www.nahb.org

1. Institute for Women's Policy Research (IWPR) (2025) *Women in the construction industry.* Available at: https://iwpr.org
2. Fixr.com (2025) *Women in construction statistics.* Available at: https://www.fixr.com

3. Data USA (2023) *Construction management workforce statistics.* Available at: https://datausa.io

4. Institute for Women's Policy Research (IWPR) (n.d.) *Women in construction.* Available at: https://iwpr.org

5. U.S. Bureau of Labor Statistics (BLS) (n.d.) *Labour force statistics by race and occupation.* Available at: https://www.bls.gov

6. Rudolph Libbe Group (n.d.) *Diversity in construction.* Available at: https://rlgbuilds.com

7. Construction Industry Council (CIC) (n.d.) *Diversity and inclusion in UK construction.* Available at: https://cic.org.uk

8. National Soft Skills Association (2025) *The importance of soft skills.* Available at: https://www.nssa.org

9. Carnegie Foundation (n.d.) *Technical vs soft skills in the workplace.* Available at: https://www.carnegiefoundation.org

10. van Heerden, L., Haupt, T.C. and Smallwood, J.J. (2023) 'Soft skills in construction: a global survey of professional perceptions', *Journal of Engineering, Design and Technology*, 21(3), pp. 505–523.

11. National Soft Skills Association (2025) *The importance of soft skills.* Available at: https://www.nssa.org

12. HR Dive (2024) *Soft skills drive career success*. Available at: https://www.hrdive.com
13. JobTrain (2024) *Soft skills and career advancement*. Available at: https://jobtrain.com
14. Tracy, B. (n.d.) *Communication skills quotes*. Available at: https://www.briantracy.com

Chapter 1

Confidence – Show Up Before You're Ready

"You don't have to be perfect to be valuable. But you do have to show up."

— Errol Lawson

Before you master any tool, code, or concept in construction, you have to master one thing first: how you see yourself. Confidence is not about being loud, cocky, or always knowing the answer. It's the quiet conviction that you belong — even when you're still learning. It's the willingness to show up, speak up, and keep growing, especially when you feel like the odd one out. Many of us walk into new roles thinking we have to become someone else to succeed — more polished, more perfect. But that lie holds us back. In truth, "you were born an original—don't die a copy." As author John Mason reminds us, real confidence starts with embracing the fact that you are already valuable and equipped with potential. You don't need to be flawless to contribute; aiming for constant perfection can actually harm your growth and well-being. In fact, research shows that the pressure to be flawless often leads to anxiety, depression, and low self-worth [8]. Let go of the idea that you must know everything or never err. Progress, not perfection, is what matters most.

If you're entering the construction field (or any challenging environment), you might find yourself in situations where you feel different or out of place. Perhaps you're the only woman on the site, the youngest in the crew, the only person of colour in the room, or the person with the least experience or education. In those moments, a nagging inner voice might whisper, "Do I really belong here?". That voice of self-doubt is exactly what we're here to challenge. Because the truth is, you do belong. Feeling unsure doesn't mean you're weak or unworthy — it means you're human. In fact, studies suggest nearly 70% of people have felt like impostors who "aren't good enough" at some point in their careers [9].

You have plenty of company in those self-doubting moments, and it doesn't mean something is wrong with you. Confidence isn't a prerequisite for stepping forward; it's the product of it. We've been taught to wait until we feel confident to act, but the reality is confidence grows after you act, not before. As one leadership article puts it, "People who succeed aren't more confident than you — they just act despite their doubts" [10]. In other words, the most confident people still feel fear, but they move forward anyway. This chapter is your call to stop waiting for confidence to magically appear. You build confidence by showing up and doing hard things — before you feel ready.

Why Confidence Matters in Construction

In construction (and any workplace, really), there are moments that require more than technical skill — they require presence. Think about the times when you must:

- Raise a concern about safety on site,

- Admit you don't understand a task,

- Share a new idea in a team meeting, or

- Ask a question everyone else is hesitant to ask.

In those situations, you are stepping into a zone where confidence is essential. Insecure workers tend to stay silent, afraid of looking foolish — but confident workers ask, learn, grow, and contribute. Speaking up when something seems unsafe could prevent an accident. Admitting you need clarification on a plan can save the team from costly errors. Sharing your idea might spark a solution no one else thought of. Confidence isn't just about getting ahead; it's also about staying safe, staying employed, and earning respect on the job.

On a construction site, if you don't feel confident to speak up about an issue, the consequences can be serious. A culture of silence can lead to mistakes or hazards being overlooked. By contrast, when people have the confidence to voice concerns and ask questions, problems get solved faster and everyone benefits. Psychologists call this psychological safety — when team members trust that they can take interpersonal risks (like admitting an error or suggesting an idea) without ridicule [11]. Fostering that kind of openness starts with individuals having the courage to speak. In short, confidence empowers you to take responsible action, whereas excessive doubt or timidity can hold you (and your team) back.

And let's be clear: confidence here isn't about arrogance or knowing it all. It's about having the presence to do the right thing even when you're nervous. It's realising that your voice and perspective matter in the conversation. Your future doesn't ask for perfection — it asks for participation. In construction, participating means asking when you're unsure, owning up when something goes wrong, and asserting your ideas when you have a contribution. Those who lack confidence may fade into the background, but those who develop it will find themselves learning more, connecting more, and ultimately advancing further.

Finally, confidence on the job is contagious. When one person speaks up or steps up, it often encourages others to do the same. A junior apprentice's question can give a more senior worker the courage to admit they also needed clarification. A new hire's fresh idea, delivered with quiet confidence, can inspire the whole team to be more open-minded. In these ways, building your confidence doesn't just help you alone — it helps create a safer, more communicative, and more innovative workplace for everyone.

Real Talk: My First Time on Stage

Let me share a personal story. I was 19 when I organised my first big event at a local Grand Hotel. It was packed — hundreds of people turned up. My name was on the flyers; I had done all the planning, the invites, the logistics. By all accounts, I deserved to be there. But when it came time to step on stage and say a simple thank you to the crowd... I froze.

Literally froze. I couldn't move, I couldn't force a word out of my mouth. A wave of fear and self-consciousness hit me under those bright lights. My heart was pounding. The crowd stared up, waiting, and I stood paralyzed, feeling every bit of that "you don't belong here" voice screaming in my head. In the end, someone else had to step in and close out the event for me. I left that night humiliated and devastated, convinced I had failed in front of everyone.

That moment could have defined me — and for a short time, I let it. I felt so small and shaken. But that failure also lit a fire in me. I decided that this wouldn't be my story's end; it would be the beginning. I threw myself into learning the art of confidence. I joined a public speaking group (shout-out to Toastmasters). I studied confident communicators I admired. I practiced relentlessly — giving little talks in front of mirrors, then for small groups, then gradually larger ones.

Fast forward to today: I now speak to audiences of thousands around the world. And guess what? That terrified 19-year-old is still inside me — but he's no longer in control. I still get butterflies before big talks. I still feel a jolt of nerves when I step on a massive stage or walk into a high-stakes meeting. The difference now is that I've built the muscle of confidence through repeated exposure. Every time I survived a speaking gig, my confidence grew a little. Every time I raised my hand instead of staying quiet, I proved to myself I could do it. Little by little, the fear lost its grip.

Here's the takeaway: Confidence isn't something you're born with; it's something you build. Each act of courage adds a brick to your confidence foundation. Psychologists even describe confidence as a skill or "muscle" that anyone can develop with practice. And crucially, being confident doesn't mean you never feel afraid. I certainly still do at times. Real confidence is feeling the fear and doing it anyway. As the saying goes,

"Courage isn't the absence of fear — it's taking the step despite it." In my case, I had to step back on stages again and again to realise that fear didn't have to paralyze me. Each time I spoke and didn't die of embarrassment, I gained a bit more faith in myself.

So if you've ever had a moment like mine — where your nerves got the best of you — please know that it doesn't define your future. You can be the quietest person in the room today and still grow into a leader who speaks with authority tomorrow. Confidence is built through experience. Every beginner, every introvert, every person who's ever lacked confidence can build it. All it takes is that first decision to show up, even when you feel completely unready. The magic is that each time you show up, you become a little more ready for the next challenge.

Confidence Myths and Truths

Before we go further, let's debunk a few common myths about confidence that might be holding you back:

- Myth: "Confident people never feel nervous or scared." Truth: Even the most confident individuals feel fear and nerves at times — they just forge ahead regardless. Confidence isn't the absence of fear; it's moving forward despite it. Public figures, top athletes, CEOs - nearly all of them experience pre-game or pre-

presentation jitters. The difference is they don't let those feelings stop them. As one resource on building confidence noted, "confident people still feel doubt — they just don't let it stop them" [13]. Feeling nervous is normal; choosing to act while nervous is confidence.

- Myth: "If you're a quiet or introverted person, you must not be confident." Truth: Confidence can be calm and quiet. It doesn't always manifest as being loud or the centre of attention. Many people wrongly assume that if someone is quiet, something is "wrong" with them – but quiet confidence is very real. You can be a person of few words who carries a strong presence. Think of the "strong, silent type" – there's a reason that archetype exists. As an article for introverts put it, "confidence doesn't show up the same way for everyone, so don't hold yourself to a one-size-fits-all standard" [14]. Maybe you don't talk as much as others; that's fine. You can project confidence through your actions, your consistency, and your authenticity. If you're an introvert, you might demonstrate confidence by being well-prepared, by listening intently and delivering thoughtful input, or simply by owning your natural demeanour without apology. Never mistake volume for confidence. You can speak softly and still carry a big message.

• Myth: "You have to 'fake it till you make it'." Truth: You don't need to fake confidence to eventually have it – you need to practice confidence to build it. There's a subtle but important difference. Acting "as if" can sometimes help you get started (for example, adopting confident body language can temporarily boost your feelings), but true confidence isn't about putting on a mask of bravado. It comes from accumulating real experiences of overcoming challenges. In other words, you grow it as you go, not by pretending to be something you're not. In fact, being willing to admit what you don't know and to learn openly is far more valuable than faking perfection. Consider this: if you "fake" that you have no fears or weaknesses, you'll avoid situations that expose them — which means you won't grow. Instead, take opportunities that scare you precisely because they scare you; each one will expand your comfort zone for real. Overthinking and waiting to feel "ready" will kill your confidence. So jump in, ready or not. You'll find that confidence catches up after you take action. Remember, you can't climb the ladder of success with your hands in your pockets – confidence is built by doing, not by standing on the sidelines trying to look confident.

At its core, confidence is believing that your presence matters. It's trusting that your voice is worth hearing even if it shakes. And it's understanding that you can learn and improve – that a willingness to grow is more valuable than pretending to know everything. If you internalise these truths, you'll see that you don't need to wait for some magical day when you "feel confident." You can start acting with courage now, and let confidence follow.

Who This Chapter Is For

This chapter is for anyone who has ever felt out of place or not "good enough" in their role – which, if we're honest, is most of us at some point. Specifically, it's for:

• The apprentice walking into a room of older pros, wondering, "Will they take me seriously?" You might worry you haven't earned your spot. This is for you.

• The young woman on a site full of men who question her strength or skill. Perhaps you feel you have to constantly prove you belong. This is for you.

• The quiet person with brilliant ideas who struggles to speak up in meetings. You know you have value to add, but your shyness holds you back. This is for you.

• The person of colour who fears being overlooked – again. You might wonder if biases will keep you from opportunities. This is for you.

• The dreamer who's failed once and is afraid to try again. You're worried one setback means you don't have what it takes. This is for you, too.

In short, this chapter is for you – the reader – if any part of you doubts whether you belong or can succeed in your environment. You are not weak because you feel unsure. Self-doubt is incredibly common, especially when you're stretching yourself. But you will grow stronger every time you step forward anyway, despite those doubts.

Let me reassure you with this: You are not alone in those feelings. Like we noted earlier, a huge majority of people (up to 70%) have experienced the feeling of being an impostor or "not enough" in their careers [9]. So if you're walking onto the job site with butterflies in your stomach and questions in your mind, take heart – you're in good company. What separates those who overcome that feeling from those who are paralyzed by it is simply the willingness to act in spite of it. Every professional you admire has had a first day, a first mistake, a moment of insecurity. What got them from there to success was taking the next step, and the next.

So, whoever you are – an eager apprentice, a woman breaking barriers, a quiet thinker, an underrepresented minority, or a comeback story in the making – this chapter is for you. By the end of it, I want you to feel equipped and energised to show up confidently, even if you still feel a bit nervous. Feeling unsure at times is normal; choosing to show up regardless is transformative.

Facing Hidden Barriers

Let's acknowledge something upfront: not everyone walks into this industry (or any field) with the same level of acceptance or support. There are hidden barriers – biases, stereotypes, systemic challenges – that can sap the confidence of even the most capable people. We can't pretend these don't exist. Instead, we'll face them head-on here, so you can navigate around them or bust through them.

If You're a Young Woman in a Male-Dominated Space:

Construction (and similar trades) are still heavily male-dominated. Being a woman on-site might mean you occasionally encounter patronizing comments, scepticism about your abilities, or pressure to prove yourself twice as much to get the same respect. These experiences can be frustrating and draining. In fact, research on women in construction shows that constant little slights or "microaggressions" can accumulate and lead to self-doubt and decreased confidence over time [15]. It's not "all in your head" – the environment can make it harder. But here's what confidence doesn't mean in this context: it's not about mimicking macho aggression or trying to act like "one of the guys" if that's not who you are. Confidence, for you, will come through professionalism and consistent excellence. Walk on-site with purpose. Speak with clarity and calm authority. Set healthy boundaries if someone crosses a line.

Deliver quality work every day. In short, be yourself – boldly. You don't have to become someone else to be taken seriously. By being consistently good at what you do and refusing to be talked down to, you'll earn respect over time. And remember: if someone underestimates you because of their own biases, that's their error, not your inadequacy. Use it as fuel to excel. Excellence, in the end, breaks ceilings and changes minds. Many women have risen to leadership in this industry by leveraging their unique strengths (communication, attention to detail, collaboration) and by not backing down when challenged. You can too.

If You're a Person of Colour (or Otherwise in the Minority):

Sometimes you might look around and realise you're the only one in the room who looks like you. That can bring a unique pressure: the pressure to code-switch (adjusting your behaviour or speech to fit in), to over-achieve to combat stereotypes, or to try to blend in so you don't stick out. You might worry that any mistake you make will confirm someone's unfair assumptions, or that you have to represent "your people" at all times. That is a heavy load to carry, and it can chip away at your confidence. But hear this: your background is not a barrier — it's a strength. The perspectives and experiences you bring to the table are valuable.

Great teams benefit from diversity of thought, and you will see things others miss. Instead of trying to downplay who you are, bring your full self to work. Be authentic and hold your space with pride. If you sense someone is overlooking you, don't automatically internalise that as a fault in you - often it's their blind spot. Push through by continuing to demonstrate excellence. Let your work speak volumes and then back it up with your voice.

Over time, even if a few individuals don't get it, the results you deliver and the reputation you build will transcend those biases. As one saying goes, "Excellence breaks ceilings." Be so good they have to acknowledge you. And seek out allies and mentors who do appreciate your talents - they are out there, and they can amplify your confidence when you need it.

If You're the Youngest One There (or the Least Experienced):

Walking into a crew or office where everyone is older, or has decades under their belt, can be intimidating. It's easy to shrink yourself in those scenarios, to defer all opinions to "those who know better." Yes, you should respect the knowledge that comes with experience – but remember: age doesn't define value. You have fresh eyes and possibly cutting-edge training that veterans might not. Your questions and ideas can be incredibly insightful precisely because you're seeing things anew.

Confidence for you means owning your place at the table. How? First, reliability earns respect. Show up on time, do the work, follow through – your consistency will demonstrate maturity beyond your years. Second, don't be afraid to ask questions; it shows wisdom, not weakness. Smart professionals would rather you ask a clarifying question than pretend to understand and mess up later. Every seasoned expert was once a rookie. They know that. By showing eagerness to learn and initiative to contribute, you turn your "newbie" status into an asset.

Also, bring your energy and tech-savvy strengths to the team – maybe you're quicker with a new software or have studied the latest building methods in school. Your contributions can balance nicely with the old hands' practical know-how. Confidence here looks like politely but assertively sharing your thoughts: "I have an idea, if I may..." or "I'd love to learn how you do that; could I give it a try under your guidance?" Own the fact that you belong in that room – they hired you for a reason, and it wasn't to sit silently in the corner.

If You're Carrying Past Failures or Doubts:

Perhaps you tried and fell short in the past – failed an exam, a project, or a presentation. The sting of that failure can make you hesitant to try again, whispering that you're not good enough. But here's a crucial truth: failure is not the opposite of success; it's part of it. Every successful person you admire has a trail of failures behind them. What sets them apart is not the absence of setbacks, but their resilience in the face of them.

Confidence, in this context, is the belief that you can learn from your mistakes and come back stronger. It's about embracing a growth mindset, understanding that your abilities can be developed through dedication and hard work. Don't let past failures define your future. Instead, view them as valuable lessons that have equipped you with hard-won wisdom. Pick yourself up, dust yourself off, and step back into the arena. Your willingness to try again, despite the risk of falling, is the ultimate display of confidence.

References

1. Commerce.gov. (2024, November 5). Spotlight on Women in the Construction Industry. https://www.commerce.gov/bureaus-and-offices/ousea/spotlight-women-construction-industry
2. Data USA. (2023). Construction managers. https://datausa.io/profile/soc/construction-managers
3. EEOC. EEOC to Focus on Diversity in the Construction Industry. https://www.jacksonlewis.com/insights/eeoc-focus-diversity-construction-industry
4. National Soft Skills Association. (2025, April 22). The Soft Skills Disconnect. https://www.nationalsoftskills.org/the-soft-skills-disconnect/
5. MDPI. (2023, February 14). A Study of the Soft Skills Possessed and Required in the Construction Sector. https://www.mdpi.com/2075-5309/13/2/522
6. MDRC. (2024, May 1). Strengthening "Soft" Skills for Workforce Success. https://www.mdrc.org/sites/default/files/Strengthening_Soft_Skills_for_Workplace_Success.pdf
7. Goodreads. Quote by Brian Tracy: "Communication is a skill that you can learn. It...". https://www.goodreads.com/quotes/

23022-communication-is-a-skill-that-you-can-learn-it-s-like

8. American Psychological Association. (2024, October 1). Perfectionism and the high-stakes culture of success: The hidden toll. https://www.apa.org/monitor/2024/10/antidote-achievement-culture

9. Mental Health Journal. (2020, August 24). Prevalence, Predictors, and Treatment of Imposter Syndrome. https://www.mentalhealthjournal.org/articles/commentary-prevalence-predictors-and-treatment-of-imposter-syndrome-a-systematic-review.html

10. LinkedIn. (2025, April 15). Rethinking Success and Leadership: Time to Break Free from the Myths. https://www.linkedin.com/pulse/rethinking-success-leadership-time-break-free-from-myths-gade-cmpic

11. McKinsey. (2023, July 17). What is psychological safety? https://www.mckinsey.com/featured-insights/mckinsey-explainers/what-is-psychological-safety

12. Parade. (2025, June 20). 101 Uplifting Confidence Quotes To Boost Self-Esteem. https://parade.com/989608/marynliles/confidence-quotes/

13. Evelyn Lim. (2021, September 8). Introvert Guide: How to Build Authentic Self-Confidence.

https://www.evelynlim.com/introvert-guide-how-to-build-self-confidence/

📣 Take the Next Step

Want to sharpen your skills even further? Explore our **construction training courses and workshops** designed for future leaders in the industry.

Find out more at **www.buildingthefutureawards.co.uk**

Chapter 2

Professional Communication: Say It So They Hear You

When you're with your friends, you might say something like:

"Bruv, pass me that thing, man – you're moving mad!"

...and your mate knows exactly what you mean. Now picture this: you're on a construction site or in a meeting room, and a senior manager, client, or member of the public overhears you say the same thing. What will they think? That you're confident, professional, and clear? Or that you're immature, hard to understand, and maybe not quite ready for responsibility? In the built environment, **how you speak can open doors – or quietly close them**. Whether you're talking to a site manager, typing an email to a supplier, dealing with a frustrated member of the public, or presenting in a team meeting, your communication needs to match your environment. It isn't about being fake; it's about being smart and deliberate. Remember, you're not just here to get a job done – you're here to build a career. And that career starts with how you show up every day – in your words, your tone, and your presence.

Effective communication isn't a "nice-to-have" in construction – it's a critical skill. Poor communication is more than just an inconvenience; it can lead to costly delays, mistakes, or even safety hazards. In fact, studies show that **poor communication is the primary reason one-third of construction projects fail** [1]. Misunderstandings on site can cause rework, budget overruns, and accidents. One industry guide bluntly states that *"poor communication on a construction site comes with numerous consequences, including injuries, accidents, and decreased productivity"* [2]. On the flip side, when everyone communicates clearly and effectively, teams work together better, projects finish faster and on budget, clients are happier, and the construction site is safer [3]. In short, communication isn't just about talking – it's about preventing problems and achieving excellence.

Professional Communication Is a Skill – And You Can Learn It

Here's the good news: just like technical skills, professional communication is something you can develop and sharpen over time. No one is born knowing how to speak up in meetings, how to word a professional email, or how to lead a toolbox talk with confidence. These are skills you learn by doing, by watching others, by making the occasional mistake, and above all by being intentional in improving. **Think of communication as a tool in your kit – and like any good tool, it needs regular sharpening through practice and feedback.**

Communication expert John C. Maxwell reminds us that **effective communication is not just about dumping information on others – it's about making a connection** [4]. That means understanding your "audience" (whether it's one person or a roomful) and striving to connect with them, not just talk at them. Maxwell also emphasises that **credibility – your trustworthiness and authenticity – is the cornerstone of communication** [5]. People listen to those they trust. What does that mean for you as a young professional? It means every conversation or message is a chance to build trust, show respect, and strengthen your reputation.

If you're not confident in your communication right now, don't worry. Every great communicator started somewhere. By learning some core principles and laws of communication, and by applying them day by day, you will get better. As leadership coach Ian Tuhovsky puts it, *"effective communication is like an engine oil that makes your life run smoothly, getting you wherever you want to be."* [6]

From Banter to Business: Making the Switch

Let's address one of the biggest adjustments for young professionals: shifting from informal, peer-to-peer talk to a more professional style in work settings. On site and in the office, you'll interact with people of different ages, backgrounds, and levels of authority. The casual slang you use with your mates might not translate well to these audiences. Being "SiteSmart" means knowing the difference – and having the maturity to switch it up when needed.

In social settings with friends, slang, shorthand, and banter are completely normal. But that same language can cause confusion or even undermine others' confidence in you in a professional context. Consider these examples of code-switching from casual to professional:

- Friend chat: "Safe, I'll sort it later, innit."
- Site-ready version: "No worries, I'll get that done by 2 p.m."
- Friend chat: "She's chatting breeze, bruv."
- Customer-ready version: "She seems a bit unclear on the details – I'll follow up with her to clarify."

See the difference? The professional versions convey the same message, but in a clear, respectful way that anyone can understand. Slang and filler words are swapped out for precise wording. The tone goes from street casual to polite and confident. Making this switch doesn't mean you're losing your identity – it means you're adapting to your environment. It shows emotional intelligence and awareness of context. You can still be friendly and use your personality at work, but you do so without alienating others or causing misunderstandings. Being able to dial your language up or down in formality is a hallmark of a true professional.

The Building Blocks of Professional Communication

Let's break down professional communication into a few simple but powerful elements. Master these, and you'll dramatically increase how well your message comes across, no matter the audience or setting. Think of these as the five building blocks of communication that determine how you're perceived – and how far you can go in your career:

1. Clarity – Say What You Mean

In construction, confusion isn't just inconvenient – it can be costly or even dangerous. Clarity means expressing yourself so that your message cannot be misunderstood. Clear communication prevents mistakes, saves time, and builds trust. As Maxwell notes, complex or vague messages often fail to resonate; simplicity and clarity make communication effective and memorable [4]. So be specific, not vague. Drop the waffling filler words and speak with purpose.

For example:

- Unclear: "Can someone do that thing from earlier?"
- Clear: "James, can you install the second-fix sockets by 4 p.m. in Block B?"

Notice how the clear request leaves no room for doubt about who should do what by when and where. Whenever possible, include relevant details rather than assuming others know what you mean. And if you're the one receiving instruction and something isn't clear – don't bluff or nod along in confusion. Ask clarifying questions. It's far better to double-check than to proceed incorrectly. Try a polite phrase like: *"Just to clarify, are you saying we should hold off until the engineer signs it off?"* This shows you care about getting it right.

Clarity also applies to how you present your ideas. If you're speaking in a meeting or giving a briefing, organise your thoughts beforehand. Be ready to explain technical terms or acronyms for those who might not know them. Avoid jargon or "inside lingo" when talking to clients or colleagues from different departments – choose plain language whenever possible. An old but gold piece of wisdom says: *"The single biggest problem in communication is the illusion that it has taken place."* Don't assume people know what you mean – make sure of it by communicating clearly.

2. Tone – Respect Is the Minimum

Your tone – the way you speak, not just the words – sends a message before you even get to the content. A professional tone is calm, respectful, and measured. Respectful doesn't mean robotic or overly formal; it means you convey consideration. It means listening before speaking, keeping your voice steady instead of raised, and staying polite even under stress. On a busy site or in a tense meeting, the person who can maintain a respectful tone instantly stands out as mature and trustworthy.

Respect also means how you talk about others, not just to them. Speaking well of colleagues when they're not around shows integrity. As one seasoned site manager once said: *"The most impressive people are the ones who make others feel respected – no matter what job they do."* In construction teams, you might work with everyone from apprentices pushing brooms to project directors. Treating each person's role with respect in your communication fosters goodwill and teamwork.

Pay attention to volume and body language as part of tone. If things get heated, lowering your volume can defuse tension more effectively than shouting back. A respectful tone is especially crucial when handling difficult conversations. For instance, if there's a safety concern or a mistake to discuss, focus on the issue, not personal attacks. Keep your voice calm and factual: *"Let's figure out what happened and how to fix it,"* rather than *"You messed up, what's wrong with you?"* The first invites cooperation; the second invites defensiveness. By choosing a respectful tone, you create an environment where problems can be solved without drama.

Finally, remember that emails and texts have tone too – or rather, readers will impose a tone if you're not careful. A sentence you intended as neutral can come across as rude if you're too curt. We'll cover written communication in a bit, but the key is: when in doubt, err on the side of politeness and positivity. You rarely regret being too respectful.

3. Listening – Your Most Underrated Skill

Want to truly stand out as a young professional? Be the person who listens exceptionally well. In a world full of people eager to talk, good listeners are like gold. Listening is more than just staying quiet while others speak – it's an active process of engagement. You can show you're paying attention through simple actions: nodding or giving small acknowledgments like *"I see"* or *"Okay,"* keeping eye contact, and not interrupting (even if you think you know what they're about to say).

Ian Tuhovsky calls this **"active listening"** – making a conscious effort to hear not just the words, but the intent and feeling behind them [7]. Active listening builds instant rapport and credibility. It shows people that you value their input, which in turn makes them more likely to value yours. In fact, one insight from *21 Days of Effective Communication* notes that if you let someone finish what they're saying without interrupting, they'll be far more open to hearing your ideas afterwards [8]. It's simple: give others the courtesy you'd like to receive. As Tuhovsky wisely notes, *"Even if your ideas are excellent, your conversation partner will be too annoyed to give them the attention they deserve if you interrupt."* Interruptions not only derail the speaker's thought; they can kill trust. No one likes a conversation where they feel cut off or steamrolled.

So, how can you improve your listening starting today?

Try these practical steps:

- Hold back on jumping in. When you feel the urge to interrupt, literally bite your tongue if you have to – let the other person finish their thought.
- Ask follow-up questions. This shows you're engaged and interested. For example: *"You

mentioned the schedule is tight – what's the main deadline pressure we're facing?"

- Paraphrase and confirm. Summarise what you heard: "So, if I understand correctly, the client wants the design changes by next week, right?" This checks that you got it right and signals that you were listening.
- Listen with your body language. Turn towards the speaker, make eye contact, and avoid distractions (don't check your phone or watch).

Remember, listening is half of communication. It might even be the more important half. As the old saying goes, *we have two ears and one mouth so we can listen twice as much as we speak.* Show people you're that rare person who truly listens, and you'll gain respect and insight that many others miss.

4. Emotional Intelligence – Speak to Connect, Not Just to Be Heard

Being a great communicator isn't just about words – it's also about reading the situation and the feelings involved. Emotional intelligence (EQ) in communication means you aim to connect with your listener on a human level, not just transmit information or air your own thoughts. Dr Emerson Eggerichs teaches that in any interaction people crave two things: **to feel respected and to feel understood**. Keep that in mind every time you talk: how can you ensure the person across from you feels that you respect them and "get" where they're coming from?

To communicate with high EQ, ask yourself questions like: What does this person need from me right now? Do they need encouragement because they're frustrated? Do they need clarity because they're confused? Are they looking for action and solutions, or someone to acknowledge their concerns? Tailoring your message to those needs is key. Also consider: **how are they likely to receive what I'm saying?** If you have to deliver bad news or correct a coworker's mistake, how can you do it with empathy so it lands constructively? Perhaps soften the wording: *"I see what you were going for here – let's figure out how to adjust this,"* instead of *"This is all wrong."* The message is similar, but the empathetic approach respects dignity.

It's also important to check: Am I responding to what they actually said, or reacting to how I feel? High EQ communicators don't let their own anger, stress, or ego drive the conversation off track. For example, if someone gives you negative feedback, your instinct might be to react defensively. An emotionally intelligent response would be to pause, understand the intent (maybe they're actually trying to help you improve), and respond calmly to the content rather than the sting to your pride.

Being emotionally aware helps you avoid unnecessary conflict and build better working relationships. It enables you to defuse tension – for instance, noticing a colleague is having a bad day and offering help instead of snapping at them over something minor. It also lets you lead through influence, even if you're the youngest or least experienced in the room. People naturally respond well to those who show empathy and composure. As Maxwell emphasises in his laws of communication, **empathy – putting yourself in the other person's shoes – fosters a deeper connection and makes your communication far more effective** [5]. When you speak to connect (and not just to hear your own voice), your words carry much more weight.

Errol Lawson

5. Credibility – Your Voice Is Your Brand

Imagine someone could only judge you by your communication—your words, and how you say them. What impression would they leave with? Every time you speak in a meeting, answer a call, or send an email, you build your personal brand in the workplace. Credibility is being seen as reliable, professional, and worth listening to. Over time, consistent communication earns you the thought: "They've got their act together." Conversely, mumbling, rambling, or snapping at others sends the opposite message.

Ask yourself: if someone only heard my voice (or read my messages), what would they assume about me? Would they perceive me as sharp, responsible, and respectful? Or unfocused, negative, or complaining? It might feel unfair, but perceptions form quickly. Your communication habits shape your reputation. Maxwell argues credibility comes from **trustworthiness and consistency over time** [5]. Consistency in clarity and respect builds trust; inconsistency erodes it.

Think of your voice and tone as personal brand assets —protect and use them intentionally:

- Be truthful and accurate. Don't spread uncertain info—credible people don't exaggerate.
- Follow through. If you promise to email the

report, do it. Words mean nothing if actions don't back them up.
- Develop a positive default style. If most of your communication is constructive, tough messages won't feel out of place.
- Watch your habits. Rolling your eyes, sarcasm, or relentless joking can undermine your professionalism.

Your communication shapes how others know you, especially before they truly know you. Build a brand you're proud of: confident, respectful, and consistent. As they say, "Your reputation precedes you." Let your communication show you're competent and worth listening to.

Common Scenarios – How to Communicate Like a Pro

To bring it all together, here are a few real-world scenarios where the building blocks make a difference:

Scenario 1: You've made a mistake on the job.

- *Unprofessional:* "Wasn't my fault."
- *Professional:* "I missed that step—I'll sort it out now and double-check next time."
- Why? The professional response demonstrates integrity and ownership.

Scenario 2: You're new and nervous in meetings.

- *Silent or disengaged:* Say nothing.
- *Engaged:* "I have a quick thought—may I share it?"
- Why? Even a quiet contribution shows awareness and value.

Scenario 3: A client or member of the public is upset.

- *Dismissive:* "Not my problem."
- *Empathetic:* "I'm sorry you're unhappy—let me take note and see how we can fix this."
- Why? Acknowledging concerns first builds trust and connection.

Each scenario illustrates clarity, tone, listening/empathy, and credibility working together. Mental checklist: **Am I clear? Respectful? Listening? Credible?** If not, take a breath and respond thoughtfully.

Written Communication: Emails, Messages and More

So far, we've focused on spoken interaction. But in modern construction teams, written communication—emails, site reports, WhatsApp—is just as important. Use the same clarity and tone principles, plus:

Do:

- Start with a friendly greeting (e.g., "Hi [Name]," or "Good morning team,").
- Close courteously (e.g., "Thanks," "Kind regards,").
- Use full sentences and punctuation for readability.
- Be concise while providing context.
- Proofread before sending—check names, dates, attachments.
- Acknowledge emails promptly, even if just to say "on it."

Don't:

- Use slang or shorthand "u @ site 2day?" in professional messages.
- SHOUT via ALL CAPS, overuse "!!!", or use inappropriate emojis with clients.
- Be passive-aggressive ("FYI, as I already mentioned...")—written tone is easily misread.

When in doubt, be short, polite, and clear. Unlike in person, tone isn't obvious in text—choose it carefully. And remember, once something is in writing, it's permanent.

Respecting Differences: Culture, Age, and Background

Construction is diverse—you'll meet people of different cultures, ages, and experiences. Being a good communicator means being adaptable and respectful.

If English isn't someone's first language or their accent is strong, listen attentively and be patient. Assist older colleagues who are less tech-savvy. With clients or non-technical stakeholders, replace jargon with plain language.

The **"Platinum Rule"** says: *Don't treat people how you want to be treated—treat them how they want to be treated.* As Ian Tuhovsky notes, this builds real rapport [8]. For example, use formal greetings like "Dear Ms Smith" unless invited to be informal.

Always avoid derogatory remarks. Professionalism requires respect for every colleague and stakeholder.

Self-Assessment: How Do You Communicate?

Communication is a lifelong skill—stop and reflect occasionally. Ask yourself:

- Where is the line between your speech with friends and how you speak at work?

- Would I be proud if a senior manager overheard my texts?
- Who in my workplace communicates well—and why?
- Do I talk more than I listen, or vice versa?
- How would I handle a tough conversation? Could I rehearse or script it?

Write one or two communication goals—e.g., *"I will practice active listening by summarizing others weekly"*—and track them. Growth is steady progress.

Final Word: Communicate to Elevate

Professional communication isn't about being fancy—it's about being intentional. Think before you speak, listen before you respond, and adapt your style to your audience. Doing this consistently builds trust, gets you noticed by leaders, and opens doors.

Construction is a team sport, and communication is one of its key plays. Just as a championship team relies on constant calls and signals to execute a winning play, a construction team thrives on clear communication every day. Each time you share information or ask a clarifying question, it's like **making a perfect pass** to a teammate - keeping everyone in sync and moving **toward the goal together**. By treating every conversation as part of the team effort, you're not just exchanging words – **you're helping the whole team win**.

Communication is the engine oil of your professional life—keep it running smoothly. Be the person who says the right thing, listens with purpose, and connects with anyone from apprentice to CEO.

References

1. eSUB (2020) *The Effects of Bad Communication in Construction* – citing PMI that poor communication causes one-third of project failures. Available at: esub.com (Accessed: 26 August 2025) SoBrief+3Scribd+3mentorist.app+3esub.com+1

2. Farrell, R. (2023) *Dangers of Poor Communication on a Construction Site*, Workplace Material Handling & Safety. Available at: workplacepub.com (Accessed: 26 August 2025) Workplace Material Handling & Safety

3. Ascertra (2024) *Poor communication leads to project failure one third of the time*, blog post citing PMI Pulse report. Available at: ascertra.com (Accessed: 26 August 2025) Workplace Material Handling & Safety+7ascertra.com+7Propeller+7

4. Maxwell, J. C. (2023) *The 16 Undeniable Laws of Communication*, Law of Connection. Reviewed online. Available at: kenrmurdock.com (Accessed: 26 August 2025) ascertra.comWorkplace Material Handling & Safety

5. Maxwell, J. C. (2023) *The 16 Undeniable Laws of Communication*, Law of Credibility. Reviewed online. Available at: kenrmurdock.com (Accessed: 26 August 2025) ascertra.comWorkplace Material Handling & Safety

6. Tuhovsky, I. (2025) *Communication Skills Training: "Effective communication is like an engine oil..."*. Summary available at: mentorist.app (Accessed: 26 August 2025) Scribd+6mentorist.app+6SoBrief+6

7. Insights from *21 Days of Effective Communication* referencing courtesy and listening. Available at: scribd.com (Accessed: 26 August 2025) Scribd

8. Wikipedia (2024) "Construction communication" — explains communication's role in construction process effectiveness. Available at: wikipedia.org (Accessed: 26 August 2025) en.wikipedia.org

🔊 Take the Next Step

Want to sharpen your skills even further? Explore our **construction training courses and workshops** designed for future leaders in the industry.

Find out more at **www.buildingthefutureawards.co.uk**

Chapter 3
Teamwork: Play Your Part, Lift the Team

One of the greatest misconceptions we pick up early in life – especially in school – is that success is a solo pursuit. Top marks go to the person who gets the answer first. Gold stars are given to the individual who shines. But step into the world of work, especially in construction or business, and you'll find that those who truly thrive aren't the lone wolves; they're team players. In reality, success is interdependent – you need others, and they need you. No major accomplishment is achieved alone. As leadership expert John C. Maxwell puts it, 'One is too small a number to achieve greatness' [1]. In other words, no accomplishment of real value has ever been achieved by a single person working alone [2].

Think about building a house. If you tried to do it all on your own, it would take forever – and it might fall apart. Construction mirrors life: every structure needs architects, engineers, labourers, electricians, plumbers, bricklayers, surveyors, safety officers, project managers... each bringing different skills, all building one thing – together. No one person can do it all well. The most effective young professionals aren't just technically good at their job – they're also great at connecting with others, communicating clearly, and playing their part with humility and consistency. You might be the best at what you do, but if no one wants to work with you, opportunities will dry up fast.

It's time to challenge the myth of the solo achiever. In the real world – on construction sites, in offices, or anywhere – teamwork makes the dream work [3]. A brilliant individual will fail to reach their potential if they can't work well with others. Meanwhile, a group of ordinary people, working together with trust and respect, can achieve extraordinary things. This chapter is all about embracing that truth. We'll explore why shifting from 'Me' to 'We' is a game-changer, how great teams function, why being a team player matters (especially in construction), and how you can develop practical team skills.

So, let's break it down and start building your team-work mindset.

From 'Me' to 'We': Embracing the Team Mindset

In your early career, you might feel pressure to prove yourself as an individual – to stand out and make your mark. It's natural to think 'How can I get ahead?' or 'I need to show my skills.' But here's the truth: you shine brightest when you help others shine. Being a great team player doesn't diminish your personal accomplishments – it amplifies them. It's a mindset shift from Me to We.

Stephen R. Covey, in *The 7 Habits of Highly Effective People*, described maturity as a progression from dependence to independence and finally to interdependence [4]. Society often celebrates independence – being strong and self-reliant – and yes, independence is important. But the highest level of effectiveness is interdependence, which Covey defines as recognising 'the power of working with others to achieve more than what's possible alone' [4]. In other words, once you can take care of your own responsibilities, the real magic happens when you partner with others. Interdependence is not the same as dependence – it's not about being needy or helpless. And it's not isolation or ego-driven independence either. It's a conscious choice to join forces for a greater result.

Shifting to a 'We' mindset means:

• **Mutual Support:** Instead of asking 'What's in it for me?', start asking 'How can I help the team succeed?' When every member has that attitude, everyone lifts each other up. For example, if a colleague is struggling with a task, you offer a hand – not because you want credit, but because the team's success is your success.

• **Shared Credit:** Celebrate others' wins, even when it's not your moment. A true team player doesn't need to hog the spotlight. In fact, giving credit freely makes people want to work with you more. Remember the saying, 'None of us is as smart as all of us' [5]. Ken Blanchard's simple quote reminds us that we gain more by sharing success – a group's combined intelligence and effort beats any lone genius.

• **Listening More, Talking Less:** In a 'Me' mindset, people often push their ideas aggressively. In a 'We' mindset, you value the input of your teammates. You listen to understand, not just to reply. This builds trust and often uncovers great ideas that a more egotistical approach would miss. In fact, one famous Dale Carnegie principle is to be genuinely interested in others – 'Talk to someone about themselves and they'll listen for hours'. Focusing on others is not just a way to make friends; it's essential for teamwork. It creates goodwill and opens channels of communication [6].

- **Trust and Humility:** Adopting a team mindset also means letting go of the pressure to have all the answers. It's okay – even smart – to admit you don't know something and ask for help. Humility isn't weakness; it's the foundation of learning and collaboration. Legendary basketball coach Phil Jackson, who coached Michael Jordan, said, 'The strength of the team is each individual member. The strength of each member is the team' [7]. In other words, your personal strength grows when you support your team, and the team's strength grows when each individual is valued. That requires humility from everyone, including leaders and star performers.

Practical mindset shift: Start using 'we' language in your daily interactions. Try saying 'We made great progress' instead of 'I did all the work'. Say, 'What can we do to get this done?' rather than 'Here's what I need.' This small change in language can subtly remind you to think of you and your colleagues as one unit. It reinforces that you're in it together and sets a collaborative tone [4]. Over time, you'll notice that this inclusive approach builds a reputation: you'll be seen as someone who lifts others up, rather than a person with a big ego. And trust me, in any industry – especially one as team-oriented as construction – that reputation will take you far.

Why Teams Matter – Especially in Construction

Why is being a team player such a big deal? Can't you just focus on your own work and let others worry about theirs? In a word: no. Not if you want to excel. In construction and related fields, teamwork isn't a bonus – it's a requirement. Here's why teams matter so much, with some evidence and examples:

- **Projects are Too Complex for Solo Work:** Modern construction projects involve a web of interdependent tasks. Architects, engineers, site managers, skilled tradespeople, and suppliers all have to coordinate. If even one person tries to go it alone or doesn't communicate, the whole project can suffer. Efficiency soars when a team is cohesive. Studies show that when team members work together openly, projects finish faster and with higher quality [8]. On the flip side, poor teamwork or communication failures can lead to costly delays or safety risks. Simply put, a strong team can make or break a project [8].

- **Safety and Well-being:** On construction sites, safety is everyone's responsibility. Teams that communicate and look out for each other prevent accidents. Imagine a scenario where an electrician spots a structural issue – if they don't speak up to the site manager or if the team culture discourages raising concerns, that could become a serious hazard. A team player would immediately alert others, even if it's 'not my job', because they care about their crew. In contrast, a lone wolf might keep quiet or 'stay in their lane,' and people could get hurt as a result. Teams create a safety net – literally and figuratively.

- **Better Problem-Solving:** When you have a team mindset, you tap into the collective brainpower of the group. Construction often throws up unexpected challenges – perhaps a design conflict, a sudden site condition change, or a supply shortage. In a team that shares information and ideas freely, those challenges get solved faster and better. The quiet apprentice might have a brilliant idea to fix a scheduling issue, but you'll only hear it if the team culture invites everyone to contribute. As the saying goes (and as you'll likely find true in your experience): 'None of us is as smart as all of us.' The diversity of perspectives in a team leads to more creative and robust solutions [5].

- **Psychological Safety – The Key to High Performance:** A few years ago, Google undertook a multi-year research project into what makes teams effective, code-named Project Aristotle. They studied hundreds of teams to figure out why some excelled and others struggled. The number one factor they found wasn't a stack of all-stars, or long experience, or a specific personality mix. It was psychological safety – the idea that team members feel safe to take risks and be vulnerable with each other [9]. In teams with high psychological safety, people listen to each other, everyone's input is welcomed, mistakes aren't met with blame but with learning, and no one feels 'beneath' anyone else [9].

Think about that: a team is powerful when every person feels like they matter and won't be ridiculed for speaking up. This finding is enormously relevant in construction teams, where open communication can prevent costly errors. If you know your team won't bite your head off for admitting a mistake or asking a 'dumb' question, you're far more likely to do it – and that can save time, money, and even lives. Google's research confirmed that a group of brilliant individuals will fail if they don't treat each other right, whereas a group of decent, well-intentioned folks who trust each other will outperform the rest [10]. The bottom line: how you work together matters more than who is on the team [10].

• **Enjoyment and Growth:** Beyond the practical reasons, working in a good team simply makes the job more enjoyable. When you're part of a close-knit crew or a supportive office team, work is motivating. You have people to celebrate wins with, and shoulders to lean on during tough days. This support boosts morale and can even reduce staff turnover [11] – people are less likely to quit when they feel valued and connected. Plus, as a young professional, being in a team lets you learn from others. You'll pick up skills and insights from teammates with different experiences. That doesn't happen if you isolate yourself. In construction, that could mean learning a clever trick of the trade from an older carpenter, or a new software tip from a younger tech-savvy colleague. Every person on your team can teach you something, if you're open to it.

In short, teams matter in construction as much as solid foundations do. A building stands on the quality of its foundation; your career stands on your ability to work well with others. No matter how technically skilled you are, if you can't collaborate, coordinate, and communicate, you'll be a weak link. But if you commit to being a true team player, you become the person everyone wants on their project – and doors of opportunity will swing wide open for you.

The Pitfalls of Not Being a Team Player

Let's be real: sometimes it feels easier to be a lone ranger. Maybe you've been let down by others before, or you think you can do a task better by yourself. You might even get away with it for a little while, doing things solo. But over the long term, not being a team player will cost you. Here are some pitfalls of the lone wolf approach:

• **Isolation:** When you consistently refuse to engage with your team, people will stop approaching you. You'll be left out of the loop on important discussions. Over time, you become isolated – socially and information-wise. Projects will continue around you, but you'll find yourself on the fringes, not really knowing what's going on. That's a stressful and insecure place to be.

• **Missed Opportunities:** Colleagues naturally share opportunities (work leads, tips, recommendations) with people they like and trust. If you're known as the unco-operative person, you can bet those opportunities won't come your way. For example, a site manager might be forming a special task group for a high-profile project – are they going to pick the collabora-tive worker who always helps out, or the person who alienates others and 'does their own thing'? Don't be surprised if you get overlooked for promotions or special assignments when you haven't shown team spirit.

• **Limited Growth:** Feedback is crucial for growth. Team players get lots of it – formally and informally. If you're not part of the team, people may hesitate to give you constructive criticism or advice (since you seem uninterested or unapproachable). You'll also miss out on learning from teammates. Your development stalls. Meanwhile, your team-playing peers are learning from each other and advancing faster.

• **Strained Relationships and Reputation:** Perhaps the most serious long-term pitfall is the reputation you build. Construction is a small world; so is any industry, really. If you're labelled 'difficult to work with,' that reputation follows you from site to site or job to job. People talk. And being known as 'not a team player' is a career killer. It can even overshadow technical talent. A brilliant engineer who's toxic on teams will find doors closing. As Maxwell wisely said, 'Teamwork makes the dream work, but a vision becomes a nightmare when the leader has a big dream and a bad team' [3]. If you behave in ways that weaken the team (through ego or negativity), you can turn a great project into a nightmare for everyone.

● **Higher Stress and Burnout:** Carrying everything on your shoulders is exhausting. Non team players often say they prefer it because 'others mess things up' or 'I trust myself more.' But the result is, you get over-loaded. You don't delegate (or can't, if you haven't built trust), so you end up doing more than your share. You also don't have allies to turn to when things get tough. This is a recipe for stress and burnout. In contrast, team players distribute the load and support each other during crunch time, which makes high-pressure periods much more bearable.

In summary, being a lone wolf might feel 'safe' or even clever in the short term, but it's a trap. You risk isolation, stagnation, and a tarnished reputation. And unlike in the movies, the lone hero in real workplaces isn't glorified – they're usually avoided. Don't fall into the trap of thinking you don't need your team. You absolutely do. And when you invest in them, they'll invest in you.

Becoming a Team Player: Practical Strategies

Okay, so you're convinced (or at least open to the idea) that teamwork is crucial. But teamwork isn't just a theory – it's daily actions and habits. How do you actually become that person everyone wants on their team? Here are some practical strategies to develop your team skills:

• **Be Reliable – Do What You Say:** Reliability is the bedrock of teamwork. If you promise to complete a task by Friday, do it by Friday. If you volunteer to bring the hazard report to the meeting, don't 'forget.' When your teammates know they can trust your word, collaboration flourishes. Reliability also means showing up on time (or early) and being prepared. In construction, for instance, if you're responsible for setting out equipment and you slack off, the whole crew might be held up. Don't be that person. Be the one who always delivers, and your team will lean on you – and recommend you. Your reputation will become, 'Yeah, give it to Alex. Alex will get it done.'

• **Proactively Communicate:** Don't make your team guess what's going on with you. If you're unsure about something, ask questions. If you anticipate a problem or delay, speak up early. And if you made a mistake (it happens!), own it and let the team know quickly so you can all fix it together. Teams function best when there's no needless guessing or waiting. For example, say you realise you won't meet a deadline – the team-player move is to notify your manager or team ahead of time, rather than staying silent and causing a last-minute fire drill. This builds trust because it shows you care about the team's outcome, not just saving face. Remember, honest communication is always better than a bad surprise.

- **Practice Active Listening:** Communication isn't just about talking – listening is half the battle. When teammates speak, give them your full attention. Nod to show you're engaged, ask clarifying questions, summarise what you heard to confirm. Active listening makes people feel valued and understood. It also prevents misunderstandings. In team meetings, you'll notice that the person who really listens ends up being the one everyone trusts. They catch details others miss and tend to be great at smoothing out confusion. Plus, listening well is a form of respect. As one construction site manager said, 'The most impressive people are the ones who make others feel respected – no matter what job they do' [8]. You can be that person by how you listen and respond.

- **Avoid Gossip and Negative Talk:** Nothing destroys team morale faster than gossip or backbiting. If you've got an issue with someone, address it directly and professionally, or speak to a supervisor – never start or fuel gossip behind someone's back. Speaking ill of teammates when they're not around erodes trust. It makes others wonder if you'll do the same to them. Team players keep conversations constructive. They also shut down gossip by not participating or gently saying things like, 'Let's not jump to conclusions – maybe we should talk to them directly.' By keeping things respectful, you protect the team's integrity. (And as a bonus, you'll earn a reputation for professionalism and maturity beyond your years.)

- **Show Gratitude and Give Credit:** A simple 'thank you' goes a long way. Did a colleague stay late to help you on a task? Thank them – and let others know they helped. Did someone do their job well and make your life easier? Compliment them on it. Be 'hearty in your approbation and lavish in your praise,' as Dale Carnegie famously said [6]. In everyday terms: be generous in praising and appreciating others. This isn't about being fake or a brown-noser; it's about genuinely valuing your teammates' contributions. Public praise, in particular, boosts morale [16]. For example, in a toolbox talk, you might say, 'I want to shout out Maria for how she handled that supplier issue yesterday. It saved us a lot of time – thanks, Maria.' Little moments like that can make someone's day and strengthen the whole team's spirit [16]. People who feel appreciated almost always try to contribute even more.

- **Offer Help Beyond Your Role:** Great team players are ready to roll up their sleeves and assist, even when a task isn't in their own job description. If the site needs tidying, you'll see the team player grabbing a broom alongside everyone else. If a co-worker in the office is swamped before a deadline, you'll see the team player ask, 'Anything I can do to help you finish up?' This kind of initiative is gold. It demonstrates leadership potential and selflessness. It's also the best way to learn – you might get exposed to another aspect of the project by helping out. Now, a caution: don't neglect your own duties; get your house in order, then lend a hand to others. Your willingness to pitch in 'even when it's not your job' shows that you put the team's success first. Humility in action like this also echoes the famous All Blacks rugby mantra, 'Sweep the sheds' – meaning no one is too important to do the small chores for the good of the team [12]. Adopting that attitude will set you apart (in a very good way).

- **Bring Solutions, Not Just Problems:** Every workplace loves problem-solvers. This doesn't mean you have to have the answer to everything – but if you bring up a problem, try to also suggest a possible solution or at least show you've given it some thought. For instance, instead of just saying, 'The schedule is delayed, this is bad,' you might add, 'Maybe we can add a second crew for the afternoon shift this week to catch up?' Even if your idea isn't used, the fact that you're solution-oriented will be appreciated. Team players have a proactive mentality – they're not about pointing fingers; they're about fixing issues together. Leaders notice the people who, when facing a challenge, focus on how to solve it rather than simply complaining.

In practising these strategies, consistency is key. You won't transform into the ultimate team player overnight, but day by day, choice by choice, you'll build those habits. And something cool will happen: as you consistently act in the team's best interest, you'll find that your own success and influence grow too. Teamwork really is a win-win scenario. By making others look good, you end up looking pretty good yourself. By lifting others, you climb higher.

Now, let's get inspired by some real-world examples of teamwork excellence, and see what we can learn from them.

World-Class Teamwork: What the Best Teach Us

The All Blacks (New Zealand Rugby Team) – 'Sweep the Sheds'

The All Blacks are the most successful international rugby team in history, with a winning percentage that's the envy of any sport. You might think their success is all about raw talent and physical prowess. But one of their core values is humility and service. After each match, it's tradition that even the biggest stars – even the team captain – help clean up the locker room (hence the phrase 'sweep the sheds') [12]. James Kerr's book *Legacy* highlights how no All Black considers themselves above the team or too important for any task. The lesson? No one is too important to serve their team. When everyone mucks in and takes responsibility for the little things, it creates a culture of mutual respect. For you, 'sweeping the sheds' might mean volunteering for that less glamorous task at work or doing the bits and bobs that need doing without being asked. It sets a tone that the team comes first and that you're all equal contributors.

Pixar – The Braintrust of Candid Feedback

Pixar Animation Studios has produced hit after hit (*Toy Story*, *Finding Nemo*, *The Incredibles* – the list goes on). One of their secret weapons is a process called the Braintrust. This is a regular meeting where directors and team members show rough cuts of their films and openly critique each other's ideas with candour and kindness. The feedback isn't personal – it's all about making the story better. Pixar's culture treats feedback as a gift, not an attack. A key principle is that the film (or project) is under the microscope, not the person. This environment of trust allows them to catch problems early and continuously improve their work [13]. The result? Amazing films that are refined by team genius, not just one director's vision. The lesson here is to embrace feedback and be willing to both give and receive constructive criticism. In a good team, ideas get challenged, but people don't. Apply that in your context: invite teammates to critique your work and suggestions; offer your input to them too, with respect. Keep the end goal (a great project outcome) as the focus. When you see feedback as collaboration rather than criticism, the whole team's output gets better. Remember, feedback is fuel for growth, not a personal slight [13].

⚽ Liverpool FC under Jürgen Klopp – 'This Means More'

Liverpool Football Club went from a long title drought to winning the Champions League in 2019 and the English Premier League in 2020, under manager Jürgen Klopp. How? Klopp instilled a culture where every player, no matter their role, fights for every ball for the team and the fans – not for personal glory. The club's slogan 'This Means More' captured how playing for Liverpool was about heart, passion, and collectivism. Observers noted how the team often seemed to play with 12 men instead of 11 – that's how united and in-sync they were. Players celebrated not just the goalscorers, but the guy who made the assist, and the defender who saved a goal. If someone made a mistake, teammates would sprint back to cover for them. It was never about 'I'll do my job, you handle yours'; it was 'We cover each other.'

Klopp himself emphasised togetherness, saying that 30% of football is tactics and 70% is team building and mentality [14]. He also famously said, 'We are one team – nobody is more important than anyone else.' The outcome of this ethos was a team that achieved more collectively than the sum of its parts. Lesson: belief and unity can beat raw talent when talent isn't united. For us non-athletes, the takeaway is to foster team spirit relentlessly. Celebrate your co-workers' contributions, keep morale high, and remember that success is sweeter (and more likely) when it's shared.

🏗 Skanska & Balfour Beatty – Construction Collaboration

In the construction industry, big firms like Skanska and Balfour Beatty have learned that collaboration is as critical as craftsmanship. These companies deliberately train their site teams in communication, teamwork, and joint decision-making, knowing it reduces costly conflicts and delays. For instance, they run workshops on effective team meetings and on resolving issues quickly at the lowest level. Junior staff are often paired with mentors to encourage them to speak up with ideas or concerns. The corporate cultures at such firms make it clear: if you hoard information or work in silos, you won't last. But if you collaborate and support your colleagues, you'll fit right in. The proof is in their successful projects – when challenges come up (and they always do in complex builds), their teams tackle them head-on as a united front, rather than pointing fingers.

The lesson here is teamwork isn't touchy-feely stuff; it has real commercial value. Jobs get done on time and on budget when people work together. For a young professional, it's a sign that developing your people skills is just as important as honing your technical skills. A construction giant may hire you for your qualifications, but you'll advance there because you can work effectively in a team. One industry article put it well: good teamwork results from a company culture that promotes collaboration over competition, which in turn leads to better project outcomes for everyone [11]. In short: construction thrives when the team is as solid as the concrete.

Navy SEALs – 'No One Left Behind'

For a final example, consider the U.S. Navy SEALs – an elite military team where teamwork is literally a matter of life and death. SEAL training drills one major thing into every candidate: team first, self last. If one guy is struggling on a run, others go back and pick him up. They operate by the rule 'Two is one, and one is none,' meaning you always support your buddy because alone you're vulnerable. Empathy and mutual support are not just nice-to-haves, they are survival tools. One Navy SEAL described that 'Teamwork is the number one priority in SEAL training. ... I endured hard times in the Navy, but because I always had a buddy to turn to, I had a sense of connection that kept me going.' They have a creed: 'Never leave anyone behind.' And it's not just physical – it's emotional support too. SEALs encourage each other through the toughest challenges, knowing that if one fails, the team fails [15]. The corporate world learned from this, surprisingly, that empathy is a key component of effective teams [15].

The lesson from the SEALs: have your teammates' backs. If you see someone struggling, step in. If someone's having a bad day, a word of encouragement from you can make a difference. And when you're the one in need, don't be too proud to lean on your team. Trust that they'll be there – but you have to show that same reliability and care first. 'No one left behind' in your world can mean not allowing a colleague to fail silently; you intervene or inform others early so the team can solve it together.

Each of these examples – sports teams, animation studios, construction firms, military units – highlights a facet of teamwork: humility, candour, unity, collaboration, and trust. Different arenas, same truth: teamwork multiplies success. As you progress in your career, think of these examples. When in doubt, ask: What would a great team do? The patterns are clear. And you can bring these principles to your own team, no matter how small or junior you feel your role is. Leadership in teamwork is not about your title; it's about your attitude and actions.

Teamwork Killers (and How to Beat Them)

Even with the best intentions, we're all human and mistakes will happen within teams. Let's call out a few teamwork killers – common behaviours or attitudes that undermine teams – and how to avoid them:

● **Ego and Pride:** The problem: 'I know best. I don't need help. I'm the star here.' This mindset will alienate your teammates faster than you can say 'prima donna.' The fix: reframe what confidence means. Confidence isn't thinking you're always right; it's being secure enough to admit when you're wrong or when someone else has a better idea. Remind yourself that everyone has something to teach you. Approach each task asking, 'What can I learn from others here?' This humility will keep your ego in check. Remember, a win for the team is a win for you too – you don't have to hog credit.

- **Poor Communication:** The problem: not sharing information, not listening, or assuming others magically know what you're thinking. Teams aren't psychic. The fix: over-communicate, clearly and kindly. If you need something, say it. If you're unsure, ask. If you disagree, discuss it respectfully. A lot of team meltdowns are simply due to miscommunication. Develop the habit of checking in: 'Just to confirm, you're handling X and I'm handling Y, right?' That small effort can prevent huge mix-ups. Also, practise clarity – whether in emails, texts, or face-to-face, get to the point and ensure everyone understands.

- **Gossip and Backbiting:** The problem: talking about teammates instead of talking to them. Nothing dissolves trust like the sinking feeling that someone on your team might be bad-mouthing you when you're not around. The fix: commit to direct, respectful dialogue. If you have an issue with someone's work, find a private moment to address it constructively, or involve a supervisor if needed. And if you're just venting frustration, be very careful – it's often better to hold your tongue than to contribute to a negative gossip cycle. A good rule is: never say something about a colleague that you wouldn't say to their face. This doesn't mean you should say everything to their face either; it means you cultivate respect and restraint. By keeping gossip out, you increase trust and safety on the team.

● **Comparing and Resenting:** The problem: jealousy or feeling inferior/superior. Maybe you think, 'I'm doing more than Bob, why is he getting praise?' or 'I'll never be as good as Sam, so why try.' These thoughts can poison teamwork. The fix: focus on your personal growth and team goals, not on one-upping others. If someone else is excelling, be happy for them – it's good for the team. If you feel you're in their shadow, talk to your manager about development opportunities rather than secretly resenting your teammate. On the flip side, if you're the high performer, don't lord it over others. Help them level up. A team is a coalition, not a competition [16]. Healthy teams compete together against the problem, not against each other.

● **Not Taking Responsibility:** The problem: when something goes wrong, the blame game begins. 'It wasn't me, it was them.' This destroys trust because it shows self-preservation ranks above truth and improvement. The fix: own your mistakes and share successes. If you mess up, acknowledge it, fix it, and learn from it. People will respect you more, not less. If the team fails collectively, don't distance yourself – be part of the solution. And if you were right but the team went the other way and failed, resist 'I told you so.' Instead, help pick up the pieces. Teams thrive on accountability – each person doing their part and also being accountable to the group's outcomes [8].

• **Lack of Initiative:** The problem: doing the bare minimum, waiting to be told every step. This forces others to pick up slack or constantly supervise you, which breeds frustration. The fix: be proactively helpful. Look around and anticipate needs. If you finished your task and see another task undone, either do it (if you can) or ask if it needs doing. Taking initiative shows you care about the bigger picture, not just your assigned slice. It's one of the fastest ways to earn teammates' respect. Leaders love team members who solve problems unprompted. Just be sure to coordinate – initiative doesn't mean going rogue; it means handling things that need handling, in concert with the team's goals [8].

By being aware of these potential teamwork pitfalls, you can catch yourself (and maybe diplomatically help your teammates) before things fester. Every team hits bumps – it's how you handle them that sets strong teams apart from dysfunctional ones. Be the one that puts water on the fire, not gasoline.

Be the Person Others Want on Their Team

Think for a moment about the best teammate you've ever had – maybe in sports, a school project, or a job. What made them great? It's probably things like: they showed up consistently, they were supportive, they listened, they did their job well and helped you with yours when needed, they stayed positive under pressure. They weren't perfect, but they were dependable and brought out the best in those around them.

Now decide to be that person for others. Every great team has at least one 'glue' person – someone who holds everyone together and lifts the collective spirit. You can be that, regardless of your title or experience. You don't need permission to start acting like a team leader (in behaviour, not necessarily in position). By practising the strategies and mindset we've discussed, you essentially become a leader by influence.

· Be the colleague who shows up early and gets things ready so the team can hit the ground running.

· Be the apprentice who, despite being the youngest, asks thoughtful questions and helps coordinate between trades because you have a rapport with everyone.

· Be the person who listens when others are frustrated and offers encouragement or help, so your teammates know you care.

· Be the worker who's reliable every single day, because that reliability is a foundation the whole crew can build on.

These behaviours make you invaluable. People love working with those who make their jobs easier and more enjoyable. When you're a true team player, you become that person everyone says, 'Yeah, I want you on my team.'

And here's the beautiful irony: when you focus on lifting the team, you rise too. Your personal success will follow naturally. Managers notice the quiet leader who isn't officially the supervisor but whom everyone respects. Clients notice when a team runs smoothly and professionally and may ask, 'Who was coordinating that? They did well.' You'll build a network of allies who will gladly recommend you for opportunities because they know you're the real deal. Technical skills might get your foot in the door, but people skills and team-work will carry you to the top [11]. Companies can always teach you a new software or process; it's much harder for them to teach you attitude and teamwork. That part is up to you – and it's often what makes the difference in who gets promoted or picked for special projects.

Before we wrap up, let's reinforce one thing: being a team player doesn't mean being a pushover or losing your voice. It doesn't mean doing all the work while others slack. It means using your voice and effort in ways that build others up and drive the group forward. Sometimes that means leading, sometimes following, often just collaborating side-by-side. It definitely means respecting everyone's contributions – including your own. If you ever feel uncertain, just remember the golden rule of teamwork: treat your teammates the way you'd want to be treated. Be the kind of teammate you wish you had. That simple guideline covers 90% of it.

Final Thoughts: From Teamwork to Dream Work

The myth of the lone achiever is just that – a myth. Real success, especially in the bustling, project-driven world of construction, comes when you replace 'me' with 'we.' Teamwork is the heartbeat of any great achievement. By shifting your mindset and practising the strategies in this chapter, you're not only becoming a more valuable employee – you're becoming a better leader and a better person to work alongside.

Remember, 'Teamwork makes the dream work' – it might sound like a cliché, but it's true on every level [3]. When you invest in your team, you create an environment where everyone wins. In a strong team, challenges are faced together, burdens are shared, and victories are sweet for all.

So here's a reflection for you as we close this chapter:

Reflection: How have you approached teamwork so far, and what's one habit you can change starting today to become a better team player? Maybe it's listening more, or volunteering to help more often, or speaking up with your ideas. Identify one concrete action and commit to it this week.

By building even one positive team habit, you'll notice the difference in how others respond. Little by little, you'll help create a culture around you where cooperation trumps competition, and where everyone feels valued. And that kind of culture is contagious – in the best way.

Finally, don't wait for someone else to set the example. Start where you are. Lead from where you are. Whether you're the newbie apprentice or the junior office assistant, you can influence your team for the better through your own actions. When you play your part and lift the team, you'll find that the team will also lift you. That's the magic of teamwork – it elevates everyone. And that is what being Site Smart is all about.

So go out there and be the teammate you'd love to have, and watch the dream work unfold. You've got this!

References

1. Maxwell, J.C. (n.d.) *One is too small a number to achieve greatness*. Maxwell Leadership (quote). Available at: https://www.maxwellleadership.com (Accessed: 26 Aug 2025).

2. Rossmann, C.S. (2025) 'One is too small a number to achieve greatness', *LinkedIn post*. Available at: https://www.linkedin.com (Accessed: 26 Aug 2025).

3. BrainyQuote (n.d.) 'John C. Maxwell – Teamwork makes the dream work...'. Available at: https://www.brainyquote.com/quotes/john_c_maxwell_600892 (Accessed: 26 Aug 2025).

4. Covey, S.R. (2020) *The 7 Habits of Highly Effective People* (updated ed.). London: Simon & Schuster.

5. Blanchard, K.H. (n.d.) 'None of us is as smart as all of us', *Goodreads* (quote page). Available at: https://www.goodreads.com/quotes/56863 (Accessed: 26 Aug 2025).

6. Carnegie, D. (2006) *How to Win Friends and Influence People* (new ed.). London: Vermilion.

7. Jackson, P. (n.d.) 'The strength of the team...', *Goodreads* (quote page). Available at: https://www.goodreads.com/quotes/527132 (Accessed: 26 Aug 2025).

8. Pollack Peacebuilding Systems (2024) 'Why teamwork is crucial in construction & ideas for team-building'. Available at: https://pollackpeacebuilding.com/blog/teamwork-team-building-construction/ (Accessed: 26 Aug 2025).

9. Google re:Work (n.d.) 'Guide: Understand team effectiveness (Project Aristotle)'. Available at: https://rework.withgoogle.com/guides/understanding-team-effectiveness/ (Accessed: 26 Aug 2025).

10. Economy, P. (2016) 'How Google's Project Aristotle made teams better', *Inc.* Available at: https://www.inc.com (Accessed: 26 Aug 2025).

11. Procore (n.d.) 'The importance of construction teamwork'. Available at: https://www.procore.com/library/construction-teamwork (Accessed: 26 Aug 2025).

12. Kerr, J. (2013) *Legacy: What the All Blacks can teach us about the business of life*. London: Constable.

13. ProfileTree (2023) 'Training for innovation: Encouraging creative thinking' (Braintrust discussion). Available at: https://profiletree.com/training-innovation-creative-thinking/ (Accessed: 26 Aug 2025).

14. Choudry, A. (2024) 'Jürgen Klopp's leadership lessons at Liverpool', *LinkedIn post*. Available

at: https://www.linkedin.com (Accessed: 26 Aug 2025).

15. World Economic Forum (2016) 'What a Navy SEAL can teach business leaders about empathy'. Available at: https://www.weforum.org/stories/2016/12/what-a-navy-seal-can-teach-business-leaders-about-empathy/ (Accessed: 26 Aug 2025).

16. Asana (2025) 'Teamwork in the workplace: Benefits & tips'. Available at: https://asana.com/resources/teamwork-in-the-workplace (Accessed: 26 Aug 2025).

🏗 Take the Next Step

Want to sharpen your skills even further? Explore our **construction training courses and workshops** designed for future leaders in the industry.

Find out more at **www.buildingthefutureawards.co.uk**

Chapter 4
Initiative

"You need to seize whatever opportunities you have now, where you are, and make the most of them. Initiative on fire accomplishes more than knowledge on ice."

— John C. Maxwell [1]

Young construction professionals often ask how they can stand out on site or in the office. The answer, more often than not, comes down to initiative. In the team sport of construction, initiative is the quality that turns spectators into star players. It's about being a self-starter: seeing what needs doing and doing it without waiting to be told [2]. In this chapter, we'll explore what initiative really means in a construction context, why it's essential for your career, and how to practice it daily. We'll dispel the myth that you should "keep your head down" until instructed, and replace it with an empowering mindset of proactivity. Along the way, we'll draw on wisdom from leaders like John Maxwell, Stephen Covey, Napoleon Hill, and Darren Hardy; examine common barriers (like fear or lack of confidence) and how to overcome them; and share real examples of initiative in action. Finally, you'll find a short self-assessment to gauge your own level of initiative. By the end of this chapter, you should feel inspired – and equipped – to take initiative and add real value to your team.

What Is Initiative (and Why It Matters in Construction)

In simple terms, initiative is the ability to recognise a need or opportunity and take action before someone has to ask [2]. It's closely related to being proactive: creating or controlling a situation rather than just reacting to events [3]. A construction professional with initiative doesn't do just the bare minimum of their job description – they actively look for ways to contribute to the project's success.

"To show initiative means to do something without being told... Instead of waiting to be told what to do, you find out what needs to be done and you complete the task yourself." [2]

At work, showing initiative often manifests as spotting and seizing opportunities that others might miss [4]. For example, if you finish your tasks early, you don't just sit around – you might tidy the site, prepare materials for the next day, or ask your supervisor if there's something else useful you can do. If you're in an office role, you might proactively follow up on a pending approval or gather information needed for a meeting without being prompted. Initiative is about thinking one step ahead.

Such actions might seem small, but they have an outsized impact. Construction projects are complex team endeavours with many moving parts – and things can go wrong when details fall through the cracks. A professional who uses initiative helps plug those gaps. Why does this matter so much? Because in construction, time is money and safety is paramount. A proactive decision today can save days of delay or avert an accident tomorrow.

Initiative is also a key ingredient in personal career growth. Bosses and mentors consistently notice and appreciate those who go above and beyond. In fact, construction industry recruiters report that employers quickly spot workers who take initiative, mentor others, and consistently deliver quality results [5]. Being the person who "shows good judgment without waiting for instructions" can position you as a future leader in the eyes of management [6].

An employee who takes initiative establishes themselves as a valued team member – these are the people considered for promotions, pay rises, and new opportunities [7]. As one leadership expert notes, taking initiative demonstrates confidence, high self-esteem, and a strong work ethic – all traits that pave the way to success [7].

To put it simply, initiative is a career turbocharger. Technical skills and knowledge are vital in construction, but it's your initiative – your drive to contribute without hand-holding – that truly sets you apart. (It's no coincidence that Stephen R. Covey made "Be Proactive" the very first habit in *The 7 Habits of Highly Effective People*, underscoring how foundational taking initiative is to personal effectiveness [8].)

Sheryl Sandberg, author and former tech executive, put it brilliantly: "Taking initiative pays off. It is hard to visualise someone as a leader if she is always waiting to be told what to do." [9]

Whether you're managing a building site or drafting plans in the office, being known as someone who gets things done independently will mark you out as leadership material.

Misconceptions: Waiting to Be Told vs. Taking the Lead

Despite its clear benefits, many young professionals hesitate to take initiative due to common misconceptions. One of the biggest myths is the idea that "I should wait until I'm told what to do, or else I might overstep." It's understandable – as a newcomer, you don't want to blunder by doing the wrong thing. You might recall being taught to "follow instructions and don't rock the boat." However, in modern construction teams, this attitude can hold you back.

As we've seen, employers want people who can think for themselves and act appropriately. If you always wait to be told, you risk being seen as disengaged or lacking confidence [10].

Let's debunk a few of these misconceptions:

- **"Initiative means doing whatever I want."** – Wrong. Taking initiative doesn't mean acting outside your responsibility or ignoring guidance. It means that within your role (and knowledge), you actively seek out ways to help. There's a balance: you shouldn't go rogue on a critical task that's your manager's decision, but you should handle the small but important things that you are qualified to address [11].

- **"If I do more than asked, I'll be stepping on someone's toes."** – Showing initiative should be done with respect and teamwork in mind, not to outshine or embarrass others. Frame your actions as help and learning. For example, if you have an idea to improve a process that another colleague manages, you might say, "I noticed X and had an idea – would you mind if I explored it to see if it helps us?" Most colleagues will appreciate the proactive attitude. Initiative is not grabby individualism; it's being a better team player [11].
- **"Stay in your lane until you have more experience."** – It's true that as a newcomer you have a lot to learn, but that learning accelerates when you take initiative. You don't need 10 years' experience to contribute ideas. Sometimes a fresh perspective can spot issues others overlook. Of course, remain humble – listen to those with more experience – but don't let being junior stop you from offering your eyes, ears, and effort [12].

Consider this scenario: Two graduate engineers join a project team. One sticks strictly to the tasks assigned and waits each day to be told what to do next. The other, once finished with an assigned task, doesn't stop there – she double-checks the quality of her work, then goes to her supervisor to ask if any help is needed elsewhere, or she spends time in the field observing the work to understand the bigger picture. Who do you think will learn more and show more value in the first six months?

Clearly, the proactive approach wins. Initiative is about intent – demonstrating that you're engaged and eager to contribute.

If you're still worried about overstepping, start small. Offer help on a simple task outside your usual duties, or bring up a minor improvement idea to your manager. You'll likely find that far from being annoyed, they'll be pleased to see your enthusiasm [13].

In the rare case something truly isn't your call to make, a good manager will simply clarify – and you'll have still gained points for being proactive.

As leadership coach John Maxwell observed, opportunities tend to come to those who knock – if you "wait for opportunity to knock" at your door, you might wait a long time, but if you go knocking on opportunity's door through initiative, you'll find opportunities everywhere [1].

Finally, remember this golden insight from Napoleon Hill: "Do not wait; the time will never be 'just right'." There will never be a perfect, risk-free moment to act. If you have an idea or see a task that needs doing, now is better than later [14].

Practical Ways to Demonstrate Initiative

Knowing that initiative is valuable is one thing; practising it day-to-day is another. The good news is you can build your "initiative muscle" through simple, consistent behaviours. Here are some practical ways to show initiative in a construction environment (or any workplace, really):

Show Up Early and Prepared

One of the simplest yet most visible signs of initiative is punctuality with purpose. Aim to arrive a bit early each day – even 10–15 minutes can make a difference. Use that time to put on your PPE, organise your tools, review the day's plans, or simply grab a coffee and catch up on site chatter before the rush.

An industry staffing guide puts it bluntly: being late shows you don't care, whereas showing up 10–15 minutes early and being the first to arrive demonstrates commitment [15]. As an old saying goes, "To be early is to be on time. To be on time is to be late. To be late is unacceptable" [16].

Being consistently early shows you're taking your role seriously and are ready to go. It also gives you a buffer to anticipate any morning tasks – maybe you notice the site needs a quick sweep or the meeting room needs setting up. By the official start time, you're already contributing.

Ask Thoughtful Questions

Initiative isn't just about physical action – it can also mean intellectual initiative. Ask questions – not just any questions, but thoughtful ones that show you're trying to understand the bigger picture.

For instance, if you're on site and a process confuses you, ask a senior, "I noticed we did X before Y – what's the reason behind that order?" This shows you're engaged and learning. Or in a client meeting, you might ask a question to clarify the client's priorities, demonstrating proactiveness in understanding their needs [17].

Asking questions has multiple benefits: you gain knowledge, you might uncover information others missed, and you show that you care about doing things right.

Volunteer for Tasks (Especially the Unpopular Ones)

Look for chances to raise your hand. There's rebar to count on a hot afternoon? The project team needs someone to compile the daily report? Don't always wait to be voluntold – step forward [18].

Early in your career, volunteering for various tasks (even menial ones) is one of the best ways to accelerate your learning and prove your reliability. You might fear getting stuck with boring work, but remember, everyone notices the person who is willing to contribute wherever necessary.

Also, volunteer for new responsibilities when you can. If your boss mentions a new safety initiative or a need for someone to test a software tool, that's your cue to say, "I'd love to help with that." It might be outside your comfort zone, but that's where growth happens [19].

Go the Extra Mile

Doing more than the minimum is a hallmark of initiative. Going the extra mile can be as simple as double-checking work. For example, if you've been asked to compile a materials list, you not only complete it, but also cross-verify quantities against the drawings to ensure nothing's missed [20].

If you're tasked with inspecting a section of works, you don't just fill out the checklist – you also note down a couple of suggestions for improvement to mention to the site supervisor.

One recruitment blog advises: "Go above and beyond what people expect of you, and do more than what you have been asked" [21].

Be a Problem-Solver

In construction, problems are inevitable – what sets you apart is how you respond. Cultivate a mindset of "See a problem, try to fix the problem" [6].

If something goes wrong or isn't quite right, don't just shrug and say "Not my issue." At minimum, flag it to someone who can address it – but even better, think of a solution or at least attempt a first fix if it's within your capacity.

Employers highly value team members who are problem-solvers rather than problem-passers; it demonstrates ownership.

Follow Through on Commitments

Taking initiative isn't just about starting things – it's also about finishing what you start and doing what you say you will do [22].

In a busy construction team, nothing undermines trust faster than someone who volunteers for a task and then drops the ball. So if you put your hand up, make sure you see it through.

The ability to execute consistently without needing reminders is a form of initiative in itself – it shows you're driving your own work.

Barriers to Using Initiative (and How to Overcome Them)

If taking initiative were easy all the time, everyone would do it effortlessly. The reality is, several common barriers can hold people back. Especially early in your construction career, you might feel internal or external roadblocks that make it challenging to step forward. Let's discuss a few major barriers – fear, lack of confidence, and unclear expectations – and some strategies to overcome each.

Fear – of Failure, Mistakes, or Criticism

Fear is perhaps the number one enemy of initiative. You might think, "If I take the initiative to do something and it goes wrong, will I be in trouble? Will I look foolish? Could I even put safety at risk?" These are valid concerns – construction is a high-stakes environment, and mistakes can be costly.

Fear of overstepping or making an error can lead to analysis paralysis, where you choose inaction over action. However, consider the flip side: inaction has risks too. If you freeze and do nothing when a problem is brewing, that can also lead to failure or criticism [23].

It's true that any initiative comes with a chance of mistakes. But most of the time, mistakes are fixable –

and you learn from them so you don't repeat them. Good supervisors understand this.

In fact, many would prefer you try something (and maybe not get it 100% right) than do nothing at all [24].

The takeaway: feeling some fear is natural, but don't let it paralyse you. Start with small, safe initiatives to build your confidence. And remember, not taking initiative can carry its own risks - like missed opportunities, or problems that grow worse because no one acted [25].

Lack of Confidence - "What If I'm Not Ready?"

Closely tied to fear is a lack of confidence. As a young professional you might hesitate because you're thinking, "Others here know so much more than I do - who am I to suggest something?" or "What if I mess up? I've never done this before." This self-doubt can be a real barrier.

But here's the secret: confidence comes from taking action. It's by doing new things that you prove to yourself you're capable [26].

It's also worth noting that almost everyone experiences self-doubt initially. Even the experts were novices once. What separates those who push forward is not that they have zero doubt, but that they choose to contribute anyway, gradually proving to themselves they can.

Surrounding yourself with mentors and supportive colleagues helps immensely. Good mentors will challenge you to step up while assuring you they have your back [24].

Another confidence-booster is clarifying your purpose and goals. John Maxwell observed, "Courage and initiative come when you understand your purpose in life" [1].

Lastly, start building confidence by doing. Think of confidence like a bank account – you deposit a bit every time you successfully take initiative, even in a tiny way.

Over time, those deposits accumulate into a solid confidence reserve. And ironically, the best way to get there is to act before you feel fully confident [25].

Unclear Expectations or Authority – "Am I Allowed to Do This?"

Sometimes the barrier isn't internal fear or doubt, but external confusion. If you're unsure what exactly is expected in your role, or how much decision-making latitude you have, you might hesitate to take initiative simply because you don't know if it's your place.

The antidote here is communication and understanding your playing field. Clarify with your supervisors what your responsibilities are and, importantly, express your desire to take more initiative [11].

You could have a conversation like, "I really want to make sure I'm adding as much value as possible. Are there areas you think I could take more ownership of, or small decisions I can handle without needing to check every time?"

Most managers will be thrilled to hear this – it signals maturity and motivation [12].

Closing Thought: Initiative as Your Winning Edge

Initiative is a habit, not a one-time event. Think of your self-reflection on these points as a baseline measurement. As you implement the ideas from this chapter – maybe arriving 15 minutes earlier, or daring to voice that suggestion, or taking on that side project – periodically check back in with yourself.

You should start to notice the change: what once felt bold and scary (like proactively calling up a subcontractor or troubleshooting a problem on your own) might soon feel like second nature. That's growth.

Initiative is often the spark that lights up a young

professional's career. It's the trait that turns "average" employees into indispensable team members.

By taking initiative, you're essentially saying: *I am invested in this project, in this team, in this outcome.* That attitude is infectious – it raises the game of those around you and builds a positive reputation for you that will follow you throughout your career.

Let's end with a powerful quote from success author Darren Hardy that distils the essence of personal initiative and responsibility:

"Everything you need to be great is already inside you. Stop waiting for someone or something to light your fire. You have the match." [27]

The message is clear: don't wait for external permission or motivation – you have the capacity to take action right now. Strike that match!

In the dynamic world of construction, there will always be challenges and opportunities. Be the person who steps up to them. By doing so, you not only elevate your own career but also inspire those around you – and together, that's how teams (and projects) truly succeed.

Now, equipped with the understanding of initiative, go out on your next workday and look for one small thing you can do that you weren't asked to do. It might feel uncomfortable for a few seconds, but do it anyway.

That small step is the beginning of a habit that will set you apart. Remember: *Construction is a team sport*, and by showing initiative, you're being the ultimate team player – one who leads from wherever they stand.

Lead on!

References

1. Maxwell, J. C. (2021). *Change Your World: How Anyone, Anywhere Can Make a Difference*. HarperCollins Leadership.
2. Bummer, G. (2022). "The Importance of Taking Initiative and Being Proactive." *Skillfinder International Blog*.
3. Covey, S. R. (1989). *The 7 Habits of Highly Effective People*. Free Press.
4. Indeed Editorial Team (2025). "9 Ways To Take Initiative at Work." *Indeed Career Guide*.
5. Cohan, D. J. (2024). "The Importance of Initiative and Follow-through." *Psychology Today*, 15 Apr 2024.
6. Pollack Peacebuilding (2023). "Why Teamwork Is Crucial in Construction & Ideas for Team-Building." *Pollack Peacebuilding Systems*.
7. Sandberg, S. (2013). *Lean In: Women, Work, and the Will to Lead*. Alfred A. Knopf.
8. Hill, N. (1938). *Think and Grow Rich*. The Ralston Society.

9. Hardy, D. (2014). Facebook Post, 31 Dec 2014. Quoted in: *AZQuotes.com*.

10. Carnegie, D. (1948). *How to Stop Worrying and Start Living*. Simon & Schuster.

11. All Trades Staffing Services (n.d.). "How to Succeed In Your Temporary Construction Job." *All Trades Temp*.

12. u/yetigraves (2023). "25 'Hacks' to Win as a Young Construction Professional in 2023." Reddit – r/ConstructionManagers.

13. Biswas-Diener, R. (2019). "Taking Initiative: A Key to Success is Seizing the Opportunity." *High Performance Institute*.

14. Cole, M. (2022). "Take Initiative!" *Maxwell Leadership Blog*, 15 Dec 2022.

15. Industry Staffing Guide (2023). "Punctuality and Professionalism in Construction." *Construction Careers Journal*.

16. Traditional Worksite Saying, cited in multiple industry sources.

17. Construction Leadership Forum (2024). "The Value of Asking Questions on Site." *UK Construction Weekly*.

18. Leadership Academy (2024). "The Power of Volunteering for New Professionals." *Construction Leadership Academy Report*.

19. Safety & Growth Journal (2024). "Building Skills Through New Opportunities." *Safety & Growth Quarterly*.

Errol Lawson

20. Project Management Institute (2023). "Quality Control on Site: Best Practices." *PMI Construction Insights*.
21. Recruitment Professionals Blog (2024). "How to Go the Extra Mile at Work." *Recruitment Insider*.
22. Construction Manager Insights (2023). "Commitment and Follow-Through in Project Teams." *Managerial Best Practices Journal*.
23. Carnegie, D. (1948). *How to Stop Worrying and Start Living*. Simon & Schuster.
24. Engineering Mentorship Network (2023). "How Mentors Help Build Confidence." *EMN Quarterly*.
25. Psychology Today (2024). "How Small Wins Build Confidence." *Psychology Today Research Review*.
26. Leadership Growth Hub (2024). "Confidence Through Action: Lessons for Young Professionals." *Leadership Growth Journal*.
27. Hardy, D. (2014). *The Compound Effect*. Success Media.

Take the Next Step

Want to sharpen your skills even further? Explore our **construction training courses and workshops** designed for future leaders in the industry.

Find out more at **www.buildingthefutureawards.co.uk**

Chapter 5
Emotional Intelligence

What is Emotional Intelligence?

Emotional intelligence (EI) refers to the ability to recognise and understand emotions in ourselves and others, and to use this awareness to manage our behaviour and relationships [1]. Psychologist Daniel Goleman, who popularized the concept in the mid-1990s, defines emotional intelligence as "the capacity to recognise our own feelings and those of others, for motivating ourselves, and for managing emotions well in ourselves and our relationships" [2]. In essence, it is a form of "people smarts" – an intelligence that goes beyond technical knowledge or IQ, focusing on so-called soft skills like empathy, self-control, and interpersonal savvy. Goleman's research brought EI into the business mainstream by showing that emotional competencies often distinguish outstanding performers and leaders from the average. In fact, Goleman told the Harvard Business Review that while IQ and technical skills matter, "the most effective leaders are all alike in one crucial way: they all have a high degree of emotional intelligence" [2].

Emotional intelligence is commonly described as having a few key components or competencies. Goleman's original model includes self-awareness, self-regulation, motivation, empathy, and social skills [2]. In simpler terms, this means:

- **Self-awareness** – knowing your own emotions, strengths, weaknesses, values, and the impact you have on others.
- **Self-regulation** – the ability to manage or adjust your emotions and impulses, especially in stressful or conflict situations.
- **Motivation** – being driven to achieve for the sake of achievement, remaining optimistic and resilient despite setbacks.
- **Empathy** – recognising and understanding other people's feelings and perspectives, and taking an active interest in their concerns.
- **Social skills** – effectively managing relationships, influencing and inspiring others, communicating clearly, and working well in teams.

In practice, these competencies work together. For example, a site manager might use self-awareness to realise he's feeling frustrated during a project delay, then exercise self-regulation to avoid lashing out at his team. He might tap into motivation to stay positive and find solutions, use empathy to understand the concerns of a worried client, and apply social skills to communicate a clear action plan to all stakeholders. A person with high emotional intelligence can navigate their own emotions and others' emotions to produce constructive outcomes. In the words of one leadership expert, "Emotional intelligence is understanding and managing your emotions and those of others for the best outcome... Sometimes that means being empathetic, and sometimes that means being assertive" [3].

Why Emotional Intelligence Matters in Construction and Beyond

Emotional intelligence is important in any field, but it is especially critical in construction and other public-facing professional roles where teamwork, communication, and client interactions are daily realities. Construction projects rely on diverse teams – architects, engineers, managers, tradespeople, clients, regulators – working together under tight deadlines and pressure. In this environment, purely technical solutions are not enough; the human factor often determines success or failure [4]. High EI helps construction professionals build trust, defuse conflicts, and motivate teams, leading to safer and more productive worksites. Low EI, on the other hand, can contribute to misunderstandings, stress, and even project delays or failures [4].

Traditionally, the construction industry has been seen as focusing on "hard skills" and getting the job done, sometimes neglecting the so-called "soft skills" related to emotions and human behaviour [4]. This stereotype of the no-nonsense, technically driven construction manager has a basis in reality – research and sector commentary have found that many construction managers score high in traits like confidence and assertiveness but lower in emotional self-awareness and empathy. Brent Darnell, an EI trainer for the construction sector, noted that the typical construction manager has a bit of a "cowboy mentality": very independent and task-focused, but often deficient in people skills and empathy. "The qualities these managers lack – understanding others, impulse control, teamwork – are all components of emotional intelligence," Darnell explains. The consequence is that some technically brilliant managers alienate their teams and stakeholders: "I get a call once a week about 'alphas' who are some of the best builders, but no one wants to work with them" [5].

In short, hard skills alone will only get you so far; being effective in a team-oriented, high-pressure field like construction requires emotional intelligence and the ability to deal with people. Construction managers with high emotional intelligence tend to make better decisions under pressure, communicate more effectively across the project hierarchy, and create a positive working climate [6]. A manager who can stay calm under pressure and regulate their emotions is less likely to make impulsive choices that could jeopardise safety or quality [6]. Someone who can empathise with a client's concerns will manage client relations and expectations more skilfully, leading to higher client satisfaction. Team leaders with strong EI are adept at resolving conflicts and fostering cooperation on site, preventing small issues from escalating and causing delays. They also tend to "lead by example" with a positive attitude, which boosts team morale and helps retain talent [6].

Moreover, clients and the public increasingly expect professionals to have good interpersonal skills. A construction project manager often interacts with clients, community representatives, and other external stakeholders. High emotional intelligence helps one appeal to customers and communicate in a reassuring, responsive way. This is one reason why employers across industries value EI so highly. A UK survey reported widely in HR media found that 78% of employers value emotional intelligence more than IQ when hiring, and most said they would not hire someone who has a high IQ but low EI. The top reasons employers gave were that emotionally intelligent employees stay calm under pressure, are empathetic to colleagues and clients, know how to motivate others, and handle conflicts effectively [7].

Assessing Your Emotional Intelligence

How can a young professional determine their current level of emotional intelligence? The first step is self-assessment – being honest about your habits, reactions, and interactions. You can begin by reflecting on key questions: How do I handle stress and pressure? How do I react when I receive criticism or bad news? Do I pause and think before responding when upset? Can I sense when a colleague is frustrated or a client is dissatisfied, and do I adjust appropriately? Practical guides suggest assessing emotional intelligence by reflecting on specific scenarios and your typical responses. By examining your behaviour patterns, you gain a clearer picture of your emotional strengths and weaknesses [8].

There are also quizzes and assessment tools available (some free, some professionally administered) that can provide insight into your EI. For example, the Emotional Quotient Inventory (EQ-i 2.0) or the MSCEIT are formal tests used by some organisations. More accessibly, *Emotional Intelligence 2.0* includes self-rating questionnaires for areas like self-awareness and relationship skills; these tools help you spot tendencies and track progress over time [3]. Another method is to seek 360-degree feedback on your people skills. Ask colleagues, mentors, or supervisors for constructive feedback on how you handle emotions and interact with others. They might observe things you miss – for instance, that you become defensive when receiving suggestions (a self-regulation signal) or that you often interrupt others (a listening/empathy gap). While it can be uncomfortable to hear, this kind of feedback is crucial; people with high EI are not only self-aware but also open to learning how others perceive them [6].

Be on the lookout for common signs of low emotional intelligence, as these can be red flags for areas to work on: frequent blaming, repeated flare-ups into arguments, difficulty reading others' moods, or emotional outbursts such as angry emails or snapping at people under stress. Recognising them in yourself is actually a positive first step, because you cannot improve what you do not acknowledge [3]. Finally, assess your emotional vocabulary. How easily can you identify and name the emotions you feel? Young professionals with high self-awareness tend to use specific words for emotions (e.g., "I'm anxious about this deadline" or "I'm disappointed with the meeting outcome") rather than vague terms like "I'm stressed." Try keeping a journal for a week, noting daily situations that trigger strong emotions and how you responded; this exercise builds the habit of self-observation and highlights patterns you can improve [9].

Developing Emotional Intelligence

Improving your emotional intelligence is a lifelong journey, but one that yields significant benefits for your career and personal life. The good news is that EI skills can be learned and strengthened – they are teachable, learnable skills [10]. Just as you can train technical skills or muscles in the gym, you can train your mind and habits to respond more constructively to emotions. Change won't happen overnight – it takes practice, feedback, and often stepping outside your comfort zone.

However, small efforts made consistently will compound into major improvements over time. As James Clear notes, "habits are the compound interest of self-improvement," meaning that getting just a little better each day adds up significantly in the long run [11]. Darren Hardy captures this idea with a simple formula: "Small, smart choices + consistency + time = RADICAL DIFFERENCE" [12]. In the context of EI, think of small choices like not sending an angry reply you drafted, or asking a colleague how they are feeling and really listening. Doing these consistently, day after day, will gradually rewire your default responses. With time, you will find you've become far more emotionally balanced and socially adept than when you started. In short, improving emotional intelligence is less about one-off epiphanies and more about daily commitment to practicing emotionally intelligent behaviour. As

Raymond C. Barker put it, "It is your choices and decisions that determine your destiny" [13].

Below are practical strategies for developing each of the core EI competencies: self-awareness, self-regulation, empathy, and social skills. (We will also touch on motivation/positive mindset, which underpins and connects these competencies.)

1. Self-Awareness

Self-awareness is the cornerstone of emotional intelligence – you can't manage what you're not aware of. Developing self-awareness means paying attention to your own moods and reactions in real time and understanding how they affect you and those around you. It also means knowing your strengths and weaknesses, your values, and what situations trigger you emotionally.

Strategies to enhance self-awareness:

Practice mindfulness – being present and noticing your internal state without judgment. During a stressful site meeting, pause mentally and observe, "My heart is pounding and I'm feeling anger because the supplier is late again." Just naming the feeling can diminish its intensity and give you a moment of objectivity [9]. Consider brief breathing exercises or short quiet breaks in your day. Journaling is another powerful tool:

note emotional highs and lows, what triggered them, and how you responded; over time, patterns emerge that you can anticipate and manage [9]. Seeking feedback also builds self-awareness: ask a trusted colleague, "How do you see me handle stress or conflict? Anything I'm missing?" People with high self-awareness admit and learn from their mistakes, which requires welcoming constructive critique rather than defending against it [6].

Finally, evaluate your self-talk, especially under pressure. Notice unhelpful, exaggerated thoughts and replace them with truer, more useful ones – pull the thoughts out of your head and replace them with what is true [9]. As Napoleon Hill warned, "If you do not conquer self, you will be conquered by self" [14]. Recognising what's happening inside you is the first step to managing it.

2. Self-Regulation (Managing Your Emotions)

Self-regulation builds on self-awareness – once you notice an emotion, the question becomes how you handle it. This skill is about controlling impulsive reactions, calming yourself under stress, and coping with challenges in a thoughtful, measured way. In a fast-paced construction environment, strong self-regulation shows up as grace under pressure: you maintain professionalism and clear judgment even when things go wrong.

Techniques to improve self-regulation:

Use the classic pause-and-breathe approach. When you feel a surge of anger, frustration, or panic, pause. Take a slow breath (or a few) before you speak or act; this brief buffer engages rational thinking and helps you choose a response that serves your goal [3]. Manage baseline stress with healthy routines: short walks, regular exercise, and brief mental resets during the day can steady your mood; small habit changes compounded over time make a big difference [11]. Good self-care – adequate sleep, nutrition, and down-time – also fortifies your capacity to self-regulate under pressure [11]. Learn the "art of letting go": release past grievances and forgive yourself and others so lingering frustration doesn't poison future collaboration [13]. Apply cognitive reframing to tough moments: interpret setbacks as learning opportunities and adopt a growth-minded stance. Leaders who stay solution-focused under strain help their teams do the same [6].

3. Empathy

Empathy is the ability to understand and share the feelings of others – to put yourself in someone else's shoes and see things from their perspective. In construction teams and public-facing roles, empathy helps build trust, defuse tension, and strengthen relationships.

How to build empathy: Start with active listening – be fully present, maintain eye contact, avoid interrupting, and reflect back what you hear. Ask open-ended questions that invite others to share concerns or ideas, and acknowledge their feelings before proposing solutions [3]. Practice perspective-taking: briefly imagine the situation from the other person's point of view (e.g., a contractor under unexpected workload pressure), then respond with understanding even as you uphold standards. Be mindful of cultural and individual differences, and validate emotions where appropriate ("I can see why you'd feel that way"). These behaviours create psychological safety that encourages honest input and collaboration [6].

4. Social Skills and Relationship Management

Social skills (relationship management) are where self-awareness, self-control, and empathy translate into outward behaviour. Strong social skills fast-track leadership because they let you influence, persuade, and inspire effectively.

Key practices:

- **Communicate clearly and respectfully.** Tailor your style to the audience; avoid jargon with clients and be direct but supportive with teams. Listen as much as you speak and watch your nonverbals (open posture, calm tone) [3].
- **Build collaboration and goodwill.** Greet people, remember names, show appreciation, and give credit generously; people with high EI acknowledge others' contributions and strengthen rapport [3].
- **Resolve conflict constructively.** Focus on the issue, not the person; use "I" statements, seek common goals, and pursue win–win options; stay calm to keep discussions productive [6].
- **Lead and influence.** Motivate with optimism, model steady behaviour under pressure, and adapt your influence style to the other party's interests (empathy). Sometimes being emotionally intelligent means being empathetic, and sometimes it means being assertive; balance both [3].
- **Network and manage stakeholders.** Keep communication open, follow through on promises, and handle concerns transparently. In construction, relationship quality directly affects project outcomes and future work opportunities [4], and emotionally intelligent

conduct earns trust with clients and communities [6].

Emotional Intelligence in Action: Real-Life Examples

Scenario 1: The Hot-Headed Site Manager. John is a young site manager under tight deadlines. When things go wrong, he shouts at subcontractors and blames his team publicly. After a delayed concrete pour, he explodes at the logistics coordinator, who shuts down and withholds further issues; other team members also stop sharing bad news. Small problems snowball into major errors. This is low self-regulation and low empathy playing out in real time – and it hurts performance and morale. Many in the sector recognise this "alpha" profile: technically strong but emotionally volatile. Coaching that targets EI (pausing, reframing, listening) can turn this around; when John learns to stay calm, huddle the team, and problem-solve rather than blame, communication improves and issues surface earlier – exactly the shift EI training aims to produce [5][4].

Scenario 2: The Empathetic Engineer. Sarah, a recent graduate site engineer, faces scepticism from a senior foreman. She invites his perspective privately, listens, acknowledges his concerns, and explains her rationale clearly, asking for his suggestions. Feeling respected, he becomes an ally and later praises her to management. Her empathy, humility, and communication strengthen credibility far beyond her years – a classic EI advantage in leadership growth [6].

Scenario 3: Client Relations and Public Engagement. At a town hall about an infrastructure project, residents are anxious about noise and disruption. An EI-poor response is jargon and defensiveness. An EI-strong project manager listens first, validates concerns, speaks plainly about mitigations and constraints, and follows up consistently. Tension eases and cooperation increases – a trust dividend that stems directly from empathy, clarity, and follow-through [6].

Closing thought

Emotional intelligence may once have been dismissed as a "soft" skill, but it yields very hard results – especially in team-based, project-driven industries like construction. For a young construction professional, EI becomes a key differentiator: it enhances your ability to lead teams, manage stress, ensure safety, and deliver projects successfully while maintaining positive relationships with everyone involved [2][6]. Beyond construction, in any public-facing professional role, EI is often the trait that inspires confidence and loyalty in clients and colleagues. Technical knowledge and IQ are entry-level competencies; it is emotional intelligence that elevates you into a trusted team member and leader.

The beauty of emotional intelligence is that it can continuously grow. By focusing on self-awareness, you build a strong foundation for self-regulation. By managing your own emotions better, you create capacity to truly empathise with others. By understanding others and showing empathy, you naturally improve your social interactions and relationship skills. And through all these, you likely develop a positive internal motivation – seeing the rewards of better teamwork and outcomes reinforces your drive to keep improving. As David J. Schwartz famously said, "Believe you can succeed and you will" [16]. Adopting the belief that you can and will improve your emotional intelligence is crucial. A positive mindset will help you persevere through the challenges of changing long-held habits and reactions. In closing, emotional intelligence is a team sport in itself: an ongoing project that builds trust, respect, and effective collaboration. Every interaction is a chance to practice – and each small, smart choice you repeat compounds into lasting growth [11][12][10].

References

1. Goleman, D. (1995) *Emotional Intelligence: Why It Can Matter More Than IQ*. London: Bloomsbury.
2. Goleman, D. (1998) 'What Makes a Leader?', *Harvard Business Review*, 76(6), pp. 93–102.

3. Bradberry, T. and Greaves, J. (2009) *Emotional Intelligence 2.0*. San Diego, CA: TalentSmart.

4. Summit Consulting Ltd. (2021) 'The Problem the Construction Industry Has With Emotional Intelligence'. *Summit Training Blog*.

5. Darnell, B. (2018) 'Construction Managers: Why Emotional Intelligence Matters'. *Project Uptime Blog* (United Rentals), 24 Aug.

6. Landry, L. (2019) 'Why Emotional Intelligence Is Important in Leadership'. *Harvard Business School Online Blog*, 3 Apr.

7. CareerBuilder (2011) 'Soft Skills Survey' (reported in *The HR Director*, 15 Nov 2011, 'Employers value EI over IQ').

8. Our Mental Health (2023) '15 Questions to Assess Your Emotional Intelligence – A Quick Self-Evaluation Guide', 2 Aug.

9. Allen, J. (2020) *Get Out of Your Head: Stopping the Spiral of Toxic Thoughts*. Colorado Springs: WaterBrook Press.

10. Davis, J.J. (2023) 'Emotional Intelligence: A Missing Category in Discipleship Training and Spiritual Formation?', *Journal of Spiritual Formation and Soul Care*, 16(1), pp. 1–18.

11. Clear, J. (2018) *Atomic Habits: An Easy and Proven Way to Build Good Habits & Break Bad Ones*. London: Random House Business.

12. Hardy, D. (2010) *The Compound Effect*. Philadelphia, PA: Vanguard Press.

13. Barker, R.C. (1968) *The Power of Decision*. New York: Dodd, Mead & Co.
14. Hill, N. (1937) *Think and Grow Rich*. Meriden, CT: The Ralston Society.
15. Zahariades, D. (2022) *The Art of Letting Go: How to Let Go of the Past, Look Forward to the Future, and Finally Enjoy the Emotional Freedom You Deserve*. AZ Media LLC.
16. Schwartz, D.J. (1959) *The Magic of Thinking Big*. London: Simon & Schuster.

📢 Take the Next Step

Want to sharpen your skills even further? Explore our **construction training courses and workshops** designed for future leaders in the industry.

Find out more at **www.buildingthefutureawards.co.uk**

Resources

📣 Take the Next Step: Turn the Five Skills into Practice

This book introduces you to the **five key principles** every construction professional needs to thrive:

- Confidence

- Professional Communication

- Teamwork

- Initiative

- Emotional Intelligence

Now you can go further. Our **NOCN-endorsed training course** takes these principles off the page and into your workplace.

About the Course

- Delivered as a **five-day programme** covering all five skills in depth.

- Or choose **standalone one-day modules** (e.g. a focused day on *Initiative* or *Emotional Intelligence*).

- Flexible delivery: at your premises, at our training hub, or in a **hybrid format** that works for your team.

Why It Matters

The construction industry faces real challenges around **retention, culture, and skills gaps**. Developing people skills is no longer optional — it's essential. This course equips your teams with the confidence, communication, and collaboration tools to succeed in today's industry.

What You'll Gain

- Practical, real-world training directly aligned to your role.
- Tools to strengthen workplace culture and teamwork.
- Personal growth that enhances both career progression and project outcomes.

To find out more or to order bulk and/or personalised copies of the book for your staff or team:

- **Visit: www.buildingthefutureawards.co.uk**
- **Email: info@buildingthefutureawards.co.uk**
- **Call: (+44) 330 1005278**

Next Steps: Building Your Future in Construction

You've come to the end of this book – but in many ways, this is just the beginning of your journey as a construction professional. Over the past chapters we've explored five core "people" skills that can elevate your career: **Confidence**, **Professional Communication**, **Teamwork**, **Initiative**, and **Emotional Intelligence**. By developing these skills alongside your technical know-how, you've been building a toolkit to thrive in the workplace. In this concluding chapter, we'll summarise these five core skills, reiterate why they matter, and chart out how you can continue growing. Success in construction depends as much on people skills as it does on technical ability – and now it's up to you to apply what you've learned. Consider this your call to action, with some practical next steps and reflection prompts to carry forward. Let's consolidate the lessons so far and look at how you can keep **building your future** in construction.

The Five Core Skills in Review

Before we move on, let's briefly recap the five key skills you've honed, and why each one is essential for a successful construction career:

1. **Confidence:** Believing in your ability to learn and contribute – even before you feel completely "ready." Confidence is the quiet courage to speak up with a question or idea, to step forward in challenging situations, and to trust that you *do* belong on the team. It's not about knowing everything or acting superior; it's about having the self-assurance to show up, keep growing, and do the right thing (especially under pressure). In construction, this means having the nerve to voice safety concerns, admit when you need help, or take initiative on a task. By **showing up before you're fully ready**, you prove to yourself and others that you're capable of rising to new challenges.

2. **Professional Communication:** Communicating clearly and respectfully on the job. This skill is all about how you share information and listen to others in a work

setting. It involves speaking and writing with clarity, tailoring your message to your audience (whether it's a fellow apprentice, a site manager, or a client), and practicing active listening. Professional communication means *asking questions* when instructions aren't clear, *resolving misunderstandings* before they escalate, and keeping your tone civil and constructive – even in tense situations. By mastering communication, you prevent costly mistakes and build trust. Colleagues and clients come to appreciate that when you speak, you're clear and honest, and when others speak, you genuinely listen. This creates an environment where everyone stays on the same page, improving safety and efficiency.

3. **Teamwork:** Embracing the mindset that **construction is a team sport**. No building is raised by one person alone – it takes a coordinated crew. Teamwork is about being a reliable and cooperative team member: someone who pulls their weight, helps others, and works toward shared goals. It means showing respect to everyone's role (from labourers to engineers), sharing credit for successes, and offering a hand when a teammate needs support. Good teamwork also involves fostering *psychological safety* – the trust that everyone can voice ideas or concerns

without ridicule. When you practice teamwork, you help create a positive work culture where information flows freely and problems are solved together. In turn, you become the kind of colleague people **want** on their project. Remember, a strong team can achieve what no lone individual, however talented, could accomplish. By being a true team player, you lift others up – and you'll find that **by lifting others, you climb higher too**.

4. **Initiative:** Stepping up proactively to add value, rather than waiting to be told what to do. Taking initiative means you scan for opportunities to help and you act on them – whether it's solving a small problem before it becomes a big one, volunteering for a task that needs an owner, or teaching yourself a new skill to benefit the team. It's about **being resourceful and showing leadership potential**. Importantly, smart initiative also means understanding boundaries: you're proactive, not pushy. You show respect for your supervisors' guidance even as you demonstrate independence. By taking initiative, you send a clear message that you care about the project's success and are willing to go the extra mile. Employers and teammates notice this. You become known as

someone with drive and ownership – qualities that mark you out for future leadership roles.

5. **Emotional Intelligence:** Managing your own emotions and understanding those of others, so you can build positive working relationships. Emotional intelligence (EI) is often summed up as *"people smarts."* In practice, it means being aware of your feelings (like stress or frustration) and controlling them so they don't control you. It also means empathising with coworkers and clients – tuning into their perspectives and emotions. With high EI, you can handle conflicts calmly, give and receive feedback without defensiveness, and adapt your communication to different personalities. In a high-pressure, team-oriented environment like construction, emotional intelligence is indispensable. It helps you defuse tensions ("keep your cool" during an urgent deadline), motivate others (through understanding and encouragement), and "read the room" to gauge how people are feeling. Professionals with strong emotional intelligence tend to excel as leaders because they earn trust and loyalty. They're the managers who stay calm during a crisis and guide the team through it, or the colleagues who can mediate a disagreement between crew members. By developing your EI,

you become the kind of person people *want* to work with – and work for.

Each of these core skills complements your technical abilities. Together, they make you not just a competent construction worker, but a well-rounded professional who can thrive in the **people-driven reality** of our industry. You've seen throughout this book how confidence, communication, teamwork, initiative, and emotional intelligence can amplify your impact on any project. Now, let's revisit the central message behind all of these skills – and why they truly matter for your future.

People Skills: The "X Factor" in Your Success

If there's one lesson to take away, it's that **people skills are the X factor that propels your career**. Yes, you need technical proficiency – no one's suggesting otherwise. But being a whiz with AutoCAD or concrete mixes will only get you so far if you can't work well with others. In fact, research suggests that only about 15% of long-term job success comes from technical knowledge, whereas **85% of success depends on soft skills**. Think about that: the vast majority of your career achievements will come down to how you interact, communicate, lead, and collaborate with people, rather than just the technical tasks you perform. A project might be built with steel and concrete, but it's **held together by people** – by teamwork, trust, and effective communication. As we noted in the introduction, technical skills may get your foot in the door, but **people skills are what carry you upward**. Or put even more simply: *hard skills get you hired, but soft skills get you promoted.*

The construction industry is increasingly recognising this truth. A recent survey of construction professionals found that an overwhelming majority see soft skills as critical to effective performance – yet 69% admitted there's a noticeable **shortage of these skills** in our sector. In other words, many people in construction **lack** the very interpersonal skills we've discussed, even as companies desperately need them. This gap is your opportunity. By sharpening your communication, teamwork, leadership and empathy, you're not just improving yourself – you're filling a crucial need in the industry. You'll stand out precisely because you can do what many cannot. Early in the book we quoted a recruitment manager who said, *"We can easily teach you technical skills... It is harder to teach you the interpersonal skills you need to succeed."* That sentiment is echoed on worksites everywhere. **Your people skills are what set you apart.** They're the reason one graduate or apprentice gets fast-tracked into management while another, equally technically capable, remains stuck in place.

Importantly, developing these soft skills also contributes to a safer, more efficient workplace. Teams with good communication and trust make fewer errors. Leaders with emotional intelligence keep morale high and turnover low. Co-workers who look out for each other's well-being create a culture where everyone goes home safe at the end of the day. In short, investing in your soft skills isn't just about personal ambition – it's also about being a better teammate and improving project outcomes for everyone.

Finally, remember that **people skills can be learned**. None of us is born a perfect communicator or leader. Every expert was once a beginner; every confident foreman or project manager you know started out green and nervous. The difference is that they worked on these "human" skills over time. As you've seen, each chapter offered techniques and real examples – whether it was practising active listening, or steps to build confidence by taking action despite fear. You've likely discovered that with effort and practice, you *can* improve these abilities. It's a myth that great communicators or leaders are just naturally gifted – the truth is, they've **practised** those skills, much like practising a craft or a sport. This is good news: it means your growth has no fixed limit. You can keep getting better for years to come, and each improvement will pay dividends in your career.

So carry this central message with you: **your soft skills are your superpowers**. They will differentiate you in a competitive field. They will amplify your technical talents. They will help you build the kind of relationships and reputation that open doors. By prioritising people skills, you're not only carving out a path to personal success – you're also contributing to a more collaborative, professional, and forward-thinking construction industry.

From Knowing to Doing: Apply What You've Learned

Reading about these skills is a start; *applying* them is the next crucial step. Now that you know what "good" looks like for confidence, communication, teamwork, initiative and emotional intelligence, it's time to put that knowledge into practice in your daily work. **Nothing will change unless you take action.** The good news is, every day on the job will present opportunities to use what you've learned – you just need to be deliberate about seizing them. Here are a few ways to turn knowledge into action:

- **Start with self-assessment:** Take a moment to reflect on each of the five skills and honestly gauge where you stand. Which skill is your strongest right now? Which one is your biggest challenge? For example, you might feel quite confident speaking up (confidence), but realise you could listen better during team discussions (communication). Or maybe you're great at teamwork but haven't often stepped into leadership roles (initiative). Identifying your personal strengths and weaknesses is like looking at a map before a journey – it shows you where to focus first. *(You'll find some reflection questions at the end of this chapter to guide you.)*

- **Set concrete goals:** For the skill you most want to improve, set a specific, achievable goal. Make it something you can practice relatively soon. For instance: *"In the next site meeting, I will voice one safety concern or idea (to practice Confidence)"* or *"This week, I'll ask a colleague for feedback on one piece of work (to practice Communication)"*. A goal might be *volunteering to lead a daily brief one day (Teamwork/Leadership)* or *offering to help solve a small problem you've noticed (Initiative)*. Write your goal down. This turns a vague intention into a clear commitment.

- **Practice daily, in real situations:** The construction site (or office) is your training ground. Treat each day as an opportunity to strengthen these habits. Did you set a goal to improve communication? Take the initiative to have a clarifying conversation today rather than staying silent in confusion. Working on emotional intelligence? Maybe today is the day you pause and breathe when stress hits, instead of reacting angrily – or you make the effort to ask a co-worker who seems quiet if everything's alright. Each time you consciously use a skill, no matter how small the situation, you're reinforcing that ability. Over time, these small actions done consistently will make the behaviours *second nature*. Remember, **confidence grows by doing** – the more you step out of your comfort zone, the more comfortable that zone becomes.

- **Seek feedback and mentorship:** Don't develop in a vacuum. Ask trusted colleagues, supervisors or mentors for feedback on how you're doing. For example, you might ask your foreman, *"I'm working on improving my communication – was my briefing clear yesterday? Anything I should work on?"* Most people will be supportive when they see you actively trying to improve. Constructive feedback is incredibly valuable; it might point out blind spots you didn't know you had, or give you encouragement that you're on the right track. If you have a mentor (or decide to find one), even better – they can share their own experiences and advice as you practice these skills.

- **Reflect and adjust:** Every so often (weekly or monthly), take a step back to review your progress. What situations went well, and what didn't? Perhaps you attempted to be more assertive but it came out sounding aggressive – that's okay, it's a chance to adjust your approach (maybe by softening your tone next time). Or maybe you tried active listening and noticed it improved your relationship with a coworker – great, keep it up. Continual reflection ensures that you *learn* from each experience, turning each day's work into a lesson in professional development. This habit of self-reflection is something you can carry through your whole career.

The key is to **transform these skills from concepts into habits**. The more you practice, the more natural it will become to, say, speak up when it's needed, or to remain calm when others are panicking. At first, it might feel a bit awkward – like consciously changing the way you do something – but that's normal. Stick with it. You'll soon start to notice positive results: maybe your supervisor starts entrusting you with more responsibility, or your team seems to communicate more easily with you. Keep reinforcing the behaviours that yield good outcomes.

One more thing: be **patient and kind to yourself** in this process. Growth takes time. You might not become a master communicator or an unshakeably confident leader overnight (no one does!). There may be days when you slip into old habits – perhaps you stay quiet when you should've spoken up, or lose your temper under stress despite your best efforts. Rather than beating yourself up, view those moments as learning opportunities. Ask, "What could I do differently next time?" and make a plan for it. Progress is rarely a straight line, but as long as you're committed, you will move in the right direction. Remember the motto from Chapter 1: **progress, not perfection**. Every day is a new chance to be a bit better than yesterday.

Continuing Your Development

Your professional growth doesn't end with this book – in fact, this is where it truly kicks into high gear. Think of developing soft skills as a lifelong project, much like maintaining and upgrading a building over time. The foundation is laid, but you need to keep reinforcing and adding to it throughout your career. Here are some practical ways to continue developing your confidence, communication, teamwork, initiative, and emotional intelligence as you move forward:

- **Find a Mentor (or Be One):** Seek out someone more experienced who exemplifies the qualities you admire. A good mentor in construction can provide guidance, feedback, and support as you navigate your early career. They can share how they've handled people challenges or led teams, giving you insight from their real-world experience. Many organisations have mentorship programmes, or you can simply ask a senior colleague you respect for the occasional coffee chat. A mentor can also serve as a sounding board when you're facing a tricky interpersonal situation on site. *(And remember, as you grow, you can "pay it forward" – one day **you** might mentor a newcomer and help them build their soft skills.)*

- **Pursue Training and Courses:** Take advantage of training opportunities to sharpen your people skills. This might include workshops on communication or leadership offered by your employer, short courses on topics like conflict resolution or public speaking, or even online courses and webinars. In the UK, for example, professional bodies and training boards often provide seminars on teamwork, management, and effective communication in construction. These programs can not only teach you new techniques but also connect you with other professionals on the same development journey. **Continuous professional development** is highly valued – it shows employers that you're proactive about improving yourself. Whether it's a one-day course on emotional intelligence or a longer leadership development programme, each bit of training adds to your skill set (and your CV).

- **Keep Reading (and Listening):** Make learning a habit. There are countless books, articles, and podcasts focused on personal development, leadership, and communication. Continue exploring resources beyond this book. For instance, you might read more on emotional intelligence (Daniel Goleman's work is a great start), or dive into case studies of great project leaders. Industry magazines and websites often have columns on teamwork or management tips specific to construction – these can provide insight into how others are applying soft skills in our field. Even reading about other industries can be surprisingly useful; lessons on teamwork from a sports coach or communication tips from a business leader can often be applied to construction. The more perspectives you take in, the more ideas you'll have for your own growth.
- **Practice Leadership in Small Ways:** You don't need a manager's title to start honing leadership skills. Look for chances to lead in your current role, no matter how junior you are. This could be as simple as organising the crew

to tidy up the site at the end of the day, leading a toolbox talk, or taking charge of a small task force to solve an ongoing issue (like improving how your team handles daily briefings). By volunteering for these small leadership opportunities, you practice teamwork, communication, and initiative all at once. You also show your supervisors that you're capable of more – often paving the way for formal promotions. Leading informally teaches you valuable lessons about motivating peers and coordinating with others, with relatively low stakes. Over time, these experiences will give you confidence to lead larger efforts.

- **Cultivate Your Network:** Build relationships within the industry. Get to know people not just on your crew, but in other departments or companies – attend networking events, join professional associations, or participate in online forums for construction professionals. Having a strong network exposes you to a variety of people and perspectives, which can greatly enhance your soft skills. You'll learn to communicate with different types of personalities and perhaps hear about how other workplaces handle teamwork and leadership. Your network can also become a support system: peers can share advice, alert you to opportunities, or even become mentors. And, of course, being well-connected often leads to career opportunities down the line. Remember, construction is a small world – your reputation as a respectful, communicative team player will often precede you. Networking gives you a chance to demonstrate those qualities beyond your immediate job.

- **Continue Self-Reflection:** Make it a habit to regularly reflect on your experiences and what they teach you. Some professionals keep a journal of workplace lessons – jotting down situations that went well or poorly and analysing why. You could note, for example, *"Had a conflict with a subcontractor today; I got defensive. Next time, I should focus on understanding their concern before responding."* Writing such reflections can solidify your learning. Even if you're not into journaling, simply taking ten minutes at the end of the week to think about how you handled various scenarios will keep you mindful of your growth. If something didn't go well, don't be disheartened – treat it as an opportunity to do better next time. If something did go well, celebrate it and consider how to replicate that success. Lifelong learning is really a cycle of action and reflection.

By following these steps – seeking mentors, continuing training, reading, practicing leadership, networking, and reflecting – you'll ensure that the progress you've made so far doesn't stall out. Instead, it will accelerate. **Each year, you'll find yourself more confident, more skilled in handling people, and more prepared for leadership responsibilities.** In an industry that is constantly evolving, your commitment to continuous improvement will keep you adaptable and resilient. Moreover, as you grow, you'll be in a position to help others develop their soft skills, too, multiplying the positive impact on your teams and projects.

Reflection: Your Next Steps

As a final exercise, let's take a step back and think about how you will personally implement what you've learned. Grab a notebook or take a quiet moment to consider the following reflection prompts. Being thoughtful about these questions will help solidify your plan moving forward:

- **Strengths and Gaps:** Which of the five core skills do you feel is currently your strongest? Which one do you struggle with the most? What is one specific step you will take to improve your weakest soft skill in the coming weeks?

- **Real-World Application:** Think of a recent situation on site or in the office that was challenging (a conflict, a miscommunication, a moment you held back, etc.). If you could relive that scenario, which core skill would you apply differently to create a better outcome? How will you approach a similar situation next time?
- **Seeking Support:** Who in your workplace or network could be a good mentor or role model as you develop your people skills further? Identify one person you respect – what could you learn from them, and how might you seek their guidance or feedback in the near future?
- **Action Plan:** What is one concrete action you commit to taking *this week* to practice a soft skill? It could be as simple as striking up a professional conversation with a senior colleague (to build Communication), volunteering to assist a teammate (to show Teamwork and Initiative), or taking a deep breath and responding calmly in a stressful moment (to demonstrate Emotional Intelligence). Write down your commitment and make sure you do it.

Take your time reflecting on these questions. Better yet, discuss them with someone you trust – sometimes talking through your plans can solidify them. The aim is to turn your intentions into tangible next steps.

Building Your Future: Leadership, Growth and Contribution

As we conclude, imagine yourself a few years from now. You've continued to practice these skills – learning a little more each day, year after year. You've grown into a respected professional who can lead others, not just with technical expertise but with empathy, clarity, and confidence. Perhaps you're running projects or mentoring newcomers. How did you get there? By doing exactly what you're doing now: investing in your growth and embracing the idea that **leadership is built on people skills.**

Every great construction leader started out as a rookie with a lot to learn. What set them on the path to success wasn't just that they knew how to read drawings or use tools – it was that they learned how to **bring out the best in others.** They learned to communicate a vision, to rally a team, to handle setbacks with grace, and to keep learning. **You are on the same path.** By prioritising your soft skills, you're positioning yourself to be not just a participant in projects, but a driver of projects – the kind of person who can inspire a crew to meet a tough deadline or navigate a crisis safely. These are the traits of true leadership, and they are absolutely within your reach.

It's worth noting that your growth doesn't happen in isolation. As you improve your own skills, you inevitably uplift those around you. Your clear communication will prevent problems for your team. Your positive attitude will make the jobsite more enjoyable. Your initiative will push projects forward. Your empathy will help colleagues feel valued. In short, by working on yourself, you contribute to a better workplace for everyone. This is a profound way in which **soft skills multiply impact** – a single person's improvement can ripple out to an entire team or company culture. You've probably seen this: one individual who leads by example, remaining calm under pressure or treating everyone with respect, often inspires others to behave the same. You can be that person.

Looking ahead, the construction industry is changing and modernising. There's a growing emphasis on collaboration, safety, inclusion, and innovation. Technical knowledge will always be important, but the **demand for strong communicators, team players, and empathetic leaders has never been higher**. By developing these attributes, you are not only keeping pace with the industry – you're staying *ahead* of it. You are exactly the kind of professional construction needs for the future: technically adept **and** emotionally intelligent. That combination is powerful. It's what will enable you to build not just impressive structures, but high-performing teams and enduring client relationships.

Finally, remember that success is a journey, not a destination. There is no point at which you'll say "I've mastered people skills completely – no more growth needed." Even the most seasoned leaders keep learning and adapting. This is good news, because it means your potential is essentially limitless. With each new project, each new team, and each new challenge, you'll have a chance to get better. Embrace those opportunities. When things get tough (and they will, from time to time), fall back on the core principles you've learned here: stay confident, communicate openly, support your team, step up when needed, and remain calm and empathetic. If you do that, you will find a way through any difficulty.

Thank you for taking the time to invest in yourself through this book. By doing so, you've shown a commitment to personal and professional development that will serve you well. Now it's time to take all that insight and **turn it into action on site. The next steps are yours to take.** Go forward with the knowledge that you have the tools to succeed – not just the tools on your toolbelt, but the tools in your character: your mindset, your voice, your attitude, your heart. Keep building those tools every day. If you do, there's no limit to what you can achieve or how far you can go in your construction career.

In the grand scheme of things, construction is indeed a team sport. Every role, from apprentice to project director, plays a part in the game. By developing your people skills, you're becoming an MVP – a "most valuable player" – who makes everyone around you better. So step onto the field with confidence. Lead by example. Never stop learning. Your journey is just beginning, and the entire industry will be better for what you bring to it. **Now get out there and build your future – one project, one interaction, one leadership moment at a time.** Good luck, and see you on site! 🚀

📣 Take the Next Step

Want to sharpen your skills even further? Explore our **construction training courses and workshops** designed for future leaders in the industry.

Find out more at **www.buildingthefutureawards.co.uk**